The HMO, Taking It All Apart, The End of a Dream

How the Insurance Companies
Took Over the HMO Field &
the Raid on FHP International
&
Preface
by
Robert Gumbiner, M.D.

Interviews Conducted
by
Sally Smith Hughes in 1996

authorHOUSE®

AuthorHouse™
1663 Liberty Drive, Suite 200
Bloomington, IN 47403
www.authorhouse.com
Phone: 1-800-839-8640

First published by AuthorHouse   1/29/2009

ISBN: 978-1-4389-3802-8 (sc)

Library of Congress Control Number: 2008911546

Printed in the United States of America
Bloomington, Indiana

This book is printed on acid-free paper.

NOTE FROM THE BANCROFT LIBRARY

Since 1954 the Regional Oral History Office has been interviewing leading participants in or well-placed witnesses to major events in the development of the managed health care or HMO movement Northern California, the West, and the Nation. Oral history is a method of collecting historical information through tape-recorded interviews between a narrator with firsthand knowledge of a historically significant event and a well-informed interviewer. The tape recording is transcribed, lightly edited and reviewed by the interviewee. The corrected manuscript is then indexed, bound with photographs and illustrative materials, and placed in The Bancroft Library at the University of California, Berkeley, as well as in other research collections for scholarly use. Because it is primary material, oral history is not intended to present the final, verified, or complete narrative of events, rather, oral history aims to preserve substantive additions to a historical record. It is a spoken account, offered by the interviewee in response to questioning, and as such, it is reflective, partisan, deeply involved and irreplaceable.

All uses of this manuscript are covered by a legal agreement between The Regents of the University of California and Robert Gumbiner, M.D., dated February 14, 1996. The manuscript is thereby made available for research purposes. All literary rights

TABLE OF CONTENTS

PREFACE

After the smoke had cleared FHP had been totally destroyed by the raiders from TakeCare, I had a period of grief for the loss of a creation that I had worked on for forty years through multiple, stressful stages so I did nothing.

A few months later I decided to do another oral history about how and why it had happened. So I called up Sally Hughes at Bancroft Library to arrange for a short oral history regarding this matter.

The oral history consisted of several conversations with Ms. Hughes and myself and her attempts to get other members of the FHP Senior Staff or Board of Directors to talk to her. However, the culprits and traitors who had participated in this execution of a proud, successful organization wouldn't talk and all she ever got was my son Burke, who of course was on my side, and our legislative analyst who was also part of our PR program who said next to nothing. So those portions will be omitted for the sake of time from the presentation.

In hindsight, I realize that I had done several things wrong in the beginning of this take over. The first was not getting a competent attorney on the case to abort it. The second was resigning from the Board after the take over. (When you leave the field you can't win the game, or putting it another way, when you leave the room you lose your power.) However, I committed another cardinal sin and that was making an important decision under severe stress, which should never have been done. If I had stayed on the Board I would have had a much better chance of avoiding this situation since my opponents were not courageous and not up for a real fight.

At the time, I was debilitated by my recent prostate surgery. It had complications, an infection, an obstruction and others. My doctors were telling me that my immune system would fail and I might die if I continued in an adversary relationship. I was weak and vulnerable, hardly able to lift up a phone, let alone make an adequate decision.

Once I learned what was going on, I should probably have cancelled my surgery and taken the time to straighten things out. But I didn't and will therefore never know whether I subconsciously allowed myself to be removed as Chairman.

In retrospect, it's hard to tell whether I would have had the energy to stop this, but perhaps, had I stayed on the Board, hired a competent attorney and let him take over, it could have been rectified, and I may have been able to save this valiant company.

But there still would have been the problem of recruiting new management and getting new board members – maybe a few "place holders," on the Board would have been helpful. I did have a couple of good candidates lined up that I had been working on for about six months, so it could have worked out.

In any event, this is as accurate of an analysis and history as I was capable of producing at that time.

INTRODUCTION

In 1990 when I retired from FHP as the CEO, I intended to stay as a traditional Chairman, dealing only with the Board of Directors (the Board meetings) and communicating with the management of FHP as a liaison for the Board. Since FHP had a lot of cash, under-valued assets, (particularly in real estate) and very little debt, I knew FHP was a big target for a take over. It was a well-run organization with management backup. We were successful, both financially and in developing and demonstrating a new type of health care delivery system.

However, I was very naive in the ways of Wall Street, particularly in regards to raiders and back-door take overs. I wanted to give my number two man, Bill Price, the opportunity to run the HMO for six months to evaluate his performance and determine whether he would retain his current position. I didn't suspect that during those six months Price would begin destroying the management and corrupting the foundation of FHP's philosophy and strategy. I knew that he was timid, indecisive, that he was not a charismatic visionary, but still, I felt he deserved a chance.

I had set up a succession plan that had failed. What I didn't realize at the time, was that most succession plans do fail because they are often foreign to the organization and have never been tried before with the individuals involved. Therefore, for a succession plan to work, you need backup succession plans, plan number two, number three and so on.

I also did not understand how devious, jealous and conniving some people can be. That there are people, people I worked with, whose ambition may not equal their ability. The less competent thought that activity could replace achievement. This eluded me; *Lesson learned.*

My advice to any CEO/founder who finds they have an emotional attachment to the strategy, mission and success of the organization, is to never abandon their position of leadership, not until they have in place someone that they know can maintain the energy, ambition and foresight to move the organization forward. Most importantly, they must find someone who truly shares their philosophy and corporate culture; *Lesson Learned.*

Somebody retiring from CEO to Chairman must also maintain the position of Executive Chairman. This would allow them to provide the final leadership and say in terms of the organization's strategic planning, organizational structure, major acquisitions, culture and vision of the future. There is no such thing as a non-executive Chairman because they will be replaced by other ambitious people; *Lesson Learned.*

Ultimately, my major weakness throughout my management career was my lack of ruthlessness. I always thought that I could get the best out of people that I would be able to motivate them to do the best they possibly could. Yet I learned, in many instances, this was not true, particularly in Price's case. When I attempted to take some pressure off him by reducing his job (but not his salary) and making an Office of the President with two people instead of one, he felt belittled and thought

I diminished his importance. From then on, Price spent the majority of his time trying to get rid of me, secretly searching for an ally to help him do this.

Remember the words of Caligula, "Don't wound your enemies, kill them." Remember the Machiavellian statement, "It's better to be feared than to be loved." I forgot these; *Lesson Learned.*

The demise of FHP can be contributed to a back-door take over by a raider. When we acquired Take Care we acquired two board members from them, which was a mistake. Their idea was not to build up FHP but to destroy it for their own financial benefit. Jack Anderson had another subconscious reason and that was that he had been a failure when working for Aetna in acquiring HMOs. He acquired two of the worst HMOs on the market, Ross Loos and another loser, which led to his termination from Aetna. So he had it in for HMOs. He was an insurance man and he wanted to prove HMOs wrong and insurance H&A right.

Some of the things that he did might land him in jail today. For instance, he decreased the capitation to the staff model medical group and then declared that they were a "money loser" so they should be spun off into a separate corporation without compensating the FHP shareholders. He spun them off all right, but he spun them off into a corporation where he and the rest of the board members, with the exception of my son Burke, were able to own most of the stock. Then they had the nerve to offer the FHP shareholders, their own asset, the staff model medical group as a separate company, with rights to buy shares in their own asset. There was a little caveat that they could only sell their shares to him and his group. That so-called failure, the operating medical group, he sold to another corporation for $80 million some four or five months later. He ripped off the shareholders but even more sophisticated Wall Street people didn't seem to understand the deal.

During this period I made several mistakes. One, I knew that Jack Anderson was lining up for a take over when he had a birthday party and invited the entire FHP Board, except Burke and myself and the board went. I didn't call him up and ask him why he did that. Next, he got rid of Mark Hacken from the Office of the President as a pre-takeover test.

There were several ways I could have gotten rid of Jack Anderson. One was to hire a decent lawyer and sue him for conspiracy since none of the objections he had to my leadership where ever voiced at a meeting. This was talked about and plotted in a conspiracy behind my back. Nothing was transparent. In addition, buried in the purchase agreement was a section that said that Jack Anderson could not become Chairman but no one on our side ever read the purchase agreement. Mr. Hacken's attorney read it but never got in touch with me, nor did Hacken since he was in on the deal. They also bought off Hacken by paying him the balance of his contract in stock options to resign from the Board an hour before the board meeting; another conspiracy.

Since Jack Anderson was a cheapskate, suing him would have probably resulted in a very quick green mail agreement with him out the door and the rest of these disloyal board members could follow. Another lesson that I belatedly learned is that, "If you have people that are disloyal, get rid of them", even if you suspect that they are disloyal. Because in the end they are eventually going to try to get you. Take decisive action early on. Get the best attorney you can get and move. *"Lesson Learned"*

Probably the major problem was I did not conceive that somebody would destroy a successful, proud, smoothly operating staff model HMO like FHP, (probably grandiose on my part). I did not understand the mentality of raiders. Their objective is to destroy a company and line their pockets by dismembering it and selling the parts.

What was left of FHP was sold for pennies on the dollar to PacifiCare. As a matter of fact, everything was sold at a fire sale; the hospital in Utah, the hospital in Southern California, the medical centers were closed and left empty. It was a disaster. If I would have known the extent of his intentions I probably would have taken a chance on my health. As a prelude, our in-house legal staff muddled through various legal anti-takeover measures without once considering a Board of Directors takeover. Lesson: start with non-voting stock for sale. Keep control.

My health was another complication. Just a week before their attack I had undergone an experimental surgery at M.D. Anderson Medical Center for my prostate cancer, which was cryo surgery– at the time very primitive and I had every complication in the book, obstruction and infection. I was so sick I couldn't lift up the telephone. My doctors were telling me that if I continued to fight these people that my immune system would fail and I would die. Given those alternatives I didn't fight very hard.

Had I known the extent of Anderson's intentions, I probably would have taken a chance on my health. Lesson: start with non-voting stock for sale; keep control.

The time for action would have been early on when I first suspected something wrong, when there was still time to get an attorney and fight. Perhaps there was a subconscious desire to get out but I didn't know how.

In hindsight, I see now that if an individual wants to be an Executive Chairman, he or she has to have their own assistant, their own financial person and their own legal advisor; all competent, all well paid, all reporting exclusively to the Executive Chairman. If the management staff hires them they may be turned against you. Be and stay ruthless! Dismiss all of the disloyal people and fill your staff and board only with those you enjoy working with. Don't let people isolate you. If you feel that they are doing so, fire them; *Lesson Learned.*

What I should Have Done

1) Not made an important decision under stress; i.e, resigning from the FHP Board of Directors.
2) Hired my own top notch attorney; i.e., the one who defended FHP against the Attorney General early when I first suspected anything.
3) Fired Price and not employed Hacken.
4) Assembled my own staff of assistants, financial and legal.
5) Sued Anderson and company for conspiracy when I was still Chairman.
6) Originally issue voting and non-voting stock. Sell only the non-voting. Keep control.
7) Buy back the voting company stock to regain control.

The rest of this small book about "The HMO, Taking It All Apart: the Raid and Its Destruction" is a limited edition, a step-by-step for those who want to know.

INTERVIEW HISTORY
--by Sally Smith Hughes, Ph.D.

In July 1996, two years after completion of his oral history,[1] Robert Gumbiner wrote me regarding a project to create an oral history "addendum". As he put it:

> The recent dramatic events within FHP which involved a backdoor takeover by the Company [TakeCare] that we [FHP] recently purchased for a premium and the betrayal of the long term Company objectives as followed for 30 years by certain Board members would be an interesting follow-up to the Oral History.[2]

The request represented an opportunity to update the previous history of FHP, a major health maintenance organization headquartered in Southern California, and also to record an example of recent trends towards consolidation and managed care in the health care field. I agreed to Dr. Gumbiner's "addendum" if the interviews were placed in the context of current changes in the HMO industry and if I could conduct short interviews with others related to the developments he wished to recount. My goal with the first request was to relate recent FHP history to the larger scene in managed care. The second request was aimed at broadening the perspective on events in which Gumbiner was a central and far-from-objective participant. I explained: "It is to your advantage and mine to produce an account that is academically credible and widely useful."[3]

Dr. Gumbiner agreed to both requests. However, the first proved easier to execute than the second. The oral history opens with Gumbiner's views on recent changes in health care policy, interlaced with references to FHP and TakeCare, the company which FHP acquired in June 1994. In relation to my second request, Gumbiner suggested the following people to contact for short interviews: Jack Anderson, Anna Marie Dunlap, Nick Franklin, Burke Gumbiner, Warner Heineman, Robert Murphy, Christine Peterson, Joe Prevratil, W. W. Price, 111, Richard Rodnick, and Ryan Trimble. All, except his son Burke, president of the FHP Insurance Division, and Nick Franklin, corporate lawyer and legislative advocate at FHP, directly or indirectly[4] refused an interview.

After discussing the refusals, Dr. Gumbiner supplied additional suggestions for interviews[5] and offered to contact them by telephone to explain the project: Gary Goldstein, Judd Jessup, and a second try for Bill Price. Once more, I issued written invitations and was again met with failure, this time total. Recognizing that other factors may also be involved, this reluctance to talk on record nonetheless provides some measure of the charged atmosphere surrounding recent changes in FHP's direction.

Oral history is an intrinsically and deliberately subjective methodology, providing one individual's (the interviewee's) view of events in which he or she has participated or witnessed directly. Although balanced against written documents and, where possible, other oral history accounts, it makes no pretense at objectivity, (if there is such a thing). This oral history is no different from any other in its reflection of the narrator's personal viewpoint. Perhaps in this volume there is merely a difference of degree. Widely known as a strong and colorful personality, Gumbiner as reflected in the interviews is strong and colorful. And at times bitter--bitter for what he sees as Takecare's destruction of his vision of FHP as a provider of quality health care at an affordable price. Evolving over the years since its foundation in the early 1960s through all the major models of health care delivery in the U.S.,[6] FHP had arrived at a combination of staff model and IPA [Independent Practice Association] which Gumbiner felt appropriate for the present health care scene.

His critics, most significantly the executives of TakeCare, disagreed. Expressed simplistically, they and others felt that many health services should be "outsourced", that is, provided by companies with which FHP contracted for services. Gumbiner's disagreement with this philosophy and disillusionment over the events following FHP's acquisition of TakeCare are the subject of this frank and revealing oral history.

INTERVIEW PROCESS

Three short interviews were conducted with Dr. Gumbiner in his new home in Long Beach, which he shares with Judy Parsons, whom he married recently. I stayed in the guest house on the adjoining property which is also the site of the art gallery housing Gumbiner's collection of Micronesian and Mexican art. The site of the interviews was Gurnbiner's office on the top floor of a building which includes his home and personal office space, including a suite for two private secretaries. We sat in a spectacular semicircular room surrounded by sculpture and artifacts and luminous views of the yacht harbor.

Still suffering from the after-effects of surgery performed on two occasions early in 1995, Gumbiner sometimes arose to pace in pain, and on another occasion curtailed the interview to consult his physician. The reader will be left to judge what affect the pain, perhaps psychological as well as physical, had on his view of history.

At Dr. Gumbiner's suggestion, Karen Rasmussen and Karen Simmons, Dr. Gumbiner's assistants, transcribed his interviews. Dr. Gumbiner edited them, and I reviewed the corrected transcripts, making some insignificant editorial changes. I decided to let repetitions stand, since to remove them would have disrupted the narrative flow and attenuated the impact of Dr. Gumbiner's insistent return to certain themes: "death of a [his] dream" for FHP, utility of a combined staff and IPA model, disillusionment with health care as a market-driven economy, and so on. Dr. Gumbiner suggested and supplied the material for the appendices. The interviews with Burke Gumbiner and Nick Franklin were transcribed and edited at the Regional Oral History Office and sent to the interviewees for review and approval.

This volume is testimony to the value--and pitfalls--of oral history conducted "in the heat of the battle". Memories and emotions, only just formed, are fresh and vivid. Accounts such as this lack the "distance" and "synthesis" characterizing most historical writing. Hence conclusions are more than ever the reader's responsibility. The difficulty is compounded when the topic, as in this case, is the rapidly changing field of health cars. The reader must judge the pluses and minuses of this variety of oral history. At the very least, she is in for an exciting account of an episode which could be taken as emblematic of the turmoil and constriction of the current health care scene.

The Regional Oral History Office was established in 1954 to augment through tape-recorded memoirs the Library's materials on the history of California and the West. Copies of all interviews are available for research use in The Bancroft Library and in the UCLA Department of Special Collections.

The office is under the direction of Willa K. Baum, and is an administrative division of The Bancroft Library of the University of California, Berkeley.

Sally Smith Hughes, PhD
Senior Interviewer/Editor

Regional Oral History Office
November 1996

February 21, 1997: Not surprisingly, history did not pause while this volume was being produced. In the final stages of processing, Pacificare began its acquisition of FHP, which state regulators approved on February 14, 1997. To chronicle the newest acquisition, Dr. Gumbiner wrote an addendum, which has been included, as he sent it, at the end of the oral history. --S. S. Hughes

ORAL HISTORY

I. THE HEALTH CARE INDUSTRY AND FHP: BACKGROUND INFORMATION

(Interview 1: February 12, 1996) ##7
The State of the U.S. Health Care Field

Hughes: The health field has changed rather remarkably in the three years since your first oral history.8 I wondered if you would care to start with your feelings about what is happening in terms of managed care, and how the [President William J.] Clinton administration policies enter in?

Gumbiner: While you were talking, I was thinking, what changes have happened? First, there have been consolidations of health provider organizations as they attempt to position themselves to be large enough to take care of larger entities and larger problems. In the last three years, we've had the Clinton administration's attempt to reconstitute the health care delivery system in order to stop the ever-spiraling upward cost of health care.

Everybody now realizes that the effort was a disaster. It was too complicated, took too long, and allowed the entrenched organizations to get ready to destroy it. This was mainly the Health Insurance Association of America, which mounted probably one of the most effective and confusing advertising campaigns in history. They worked on the theory that, if you can't defeat them, confuse them. So the American public became so confused that, although most of them want something done about rising health care costs and the disorganized way it is being delivered, they couldn't figure out the administration's plan.

I was on the side of just expanding Medicare to take in pregnant women and children and lower the Medicare eligible age to fifty-five; then we could slowly and incrementally include the entire population. We have had Medicare for almost twenty-four or twenty-five years now, and had a chance to shake out a lot of problems.

At the same time, we have had quite a Republican congressional revolution during the last year. Approximately a year ago, the Republican right wing got control of both the [U.S.] Senate and the [U.S.] House [of Representatives]. The House began working to get rid of the so-called social safety net. I don't think they have gotten any place because we now see they can't really do anything to Medicare, and it's now a budget standoff. This really is a standoff in philosophy between Clinton--his administration wants to preserve the safety nets of Medicare and Medicaid--and the Republican House, with Speaker Newt Gingrich, who wants to diminish them.

Again, we have a confusing situation where the House claims that they are not diminishing benefits and the administration says they are. But if you analyze it, you realize that the amount of money that the House wants to allocate over the next seven years is not enough to support the present level of benefits. It's as simple as that. Although it looks like a lot money, it won't do it.

Putting Medicaid back to the states in block grants is another idea. That won't work either, because we all know many of the states don't have the capacity to administrate a state program well. That has been proven in the Medicaid program and some of the other programs. They just don't have the ability to do it. And the closer you get to the local courthouse, the more strange things happen. As the Chinese say, "The more eyes that are watching, the less strange things happen." And we do have more eyes in Washington.

We also have had the congressional direction to be leaner, meaner, more greedy, less altruistic and with less social consciousness. That has been pushed by the Republican majority in the House and to some extent in the Senate. This, in my view, sort of trickles down to the whole business community. There are a lot of business people, bean counters, money grubbers, and people who really don't care about anything except lining their own pockets, who have taken this government attitude to demonstrate greed, not caring about their customers or the people who work for them. It used to be--and we all know that this is nothing new--that you could expect to work for a company for the rest of your life if you did a good job. Nowadays they estimate that the average person will work for ten different companies during their career. It's as if there is a go ahead for "greed is good".

I was looking at a cartoon from the New Yorker. One man is looking at the other and says, "Yes, the fact that you have been an outstanding employee for twenty-five years is going to look great on your resume." That is the attitude that has developed in the last three years.

There is another cartoon here from the International Herald Tribune that shows the chairman of the board and the president, just the two of them in the board room, and they have a chart that shows the number of employees going down and the profits going up. There is a big sign saying "DOWNSIZING". Then the chairman says to the president, "The downside, of course, is it's your turn to clean the men's room."

Opinion letters and editorials are starting to come out, in which people are beginning to realize that this whole idea of "re-engineering," "downsizing," "outsourcing," and all of the cute little words and gibberish that they put on these new-style gimmicks, are not productive and represent poor management. These fads will go away, because anybody that knows anything about good management knows that a manager's job is to constantly build their staff. They bring in better people, move people on that no longer measure up, and redesign their table of organization. So "restructure" is not a new word. It's just a word for firing loyal employees and cutting your company down to where it cannot grow but makes more profit in the short run.

I have always been of the opinion that in order for a company to grow, you have to have many more people than are needed to operate the existing company, particularly in management. You need the extra capacity to get today's work done plus the work done in management to expand and develop. It's like allocating money for research and development. These people that are into the restructuring craze are cutting out all of the research and development because that does not make the shareholders any money short-term. So research and development, public relations, advertising, marketing, and management training are going by the wayside.

Hughes: What about good medicine?

Gumbiner: Well, what about it?

Hughes: Where does it fit into this scheme?

Gumbiner: It doesn't fit at all in the scheme of folks who are interested in simply maximizing shareholders' return. This fellow that took over from me [as chairman of the board of directors of FHP], Jack Anderson, is strictly an investor. He was an insurance executive; that is the best he has ever done. As far as I could find out, he has no experience in managing anything, although at one time he worked for Aetna, theoretically being in charge of bringing Aetna into the HMO [health maintenance organization] business. As I recall, at that time they bought the two sickest HMOs in the country and did nothing but consistently lose money in the HMO business. They were a joke in the industry.

One of my mistakes in the TakeCare acquisition was not investigating Mr. Anderson thoroughly enough to find out what his background was. I tried it, but I didn't seem to get very far in my inquiring. Probably as a word to the wise, anybody expecting to take over a company should pay more attention to the due diligence, to the point of hiring a financial investigating firm to find out exactly what the person's history is, where they have been, and what they did. I will get into that whole thing later.

Hughes: Do you think that your failure to thoroughly investigate Anderson, and perhaps others in TakeCare, was because at that stage you were expecting to fold TakeCare into FHP and, therefore, it wouldn't be quite as critical who the TakeCare people were?

Gumbiner: That is part of it. We were acquiring TakeCare. I should have been somewhat suspicious when Anderson wanted two seats on our board. At the time, we had nine board members. I thought that two seats out of nine would be reasonably safe. But I didn't calculate on how insidious and ruthless one individual can get. They bide their time and wait until people resign, or their target loses focus and gets ill as I did, or they find a jealous or resentful board member. If you go back to some of Machiavelli's writings, he said, "When you take over a country, you kill the ruling family." I think that Anderson expected me to do that, because part of the deal was the golden parachute for his ten senior executives. If he had taken us over, he would have executed our people, as he actually did when he replaced me.

I failed to remove the TakeCare executives because I thought that we could merge these two companies, acquire their better managers, and together build a bigger and more successful company. I naively thought Anderson would join me in helping me build a bigger and better company, and that is why I made him chairman of the Audit and Finance Committee.

FHP Presence in Washington and Sacramento[9]

Hughes: Let's not get into the details of that quite yet, because I still want to paint this broader picture in a bit more detail. You told me in our previous interviews that FHP had legislative offices in both Washington [D.C.] and in Sacramento [California state capital]. Did those offices play any significant role in this move towards health reform?

Gumbiner: I was always of the opinion that, if you are in the health care movement or business, which is very politicized, you must be represented in Washington and Sacramento, since the majority of health care in this country is being paid for by the federal or state government, when you take into account the huge Medicare expenditures, Medicaid, federal employees, state employees, et cetera. Health care is such a sensitive topic politically that we have had round after round of people trying to do something about health care expenditures and coverage for everybody. FDR [President Franklin D. Roosevelt] tried it, [President Harry S.] Truman tried it, and if I recall correctly, [President Richard M.] Nixon tried it. It never got any place against the entrenched political-medical establishment.

I felt that any organization of any size that is dealing with the federal government, or state and local government, in providing health care really has to have representation in Washington, and in our case also in California, since it is such a big state. If nothing else, the legislative office simply keeps the organization aware of what is happening on the legislative front so that they don't suddenly wake up some day and find out that some cataclysmic piece of legislation has just been passed that is either a deterrent to their ability to supply health care or is even threatening to the life of the organization.

Obviously, the senators and congressmen cannot read all of the bills that are put on their desks, nor understand them. Thousands of bills come across their desks annually. Even their staff can't read them all, no matter how big their staff is. So they do depend upon the lobbyists that work for different companies to give them a specialized opinion.

So not only is the legislative office responsible for keeping the company aware of what is happening in a defensive manner, but also they can be a progressive component of helping the legislators understand what the basic problems are in various legislative proposals.

In answer to your question, our office played no role because the administration stonewalled any advice or representation from the industry and, incidentally, they failed.

Hughes: Do you remember when FHP opened lobbying offices?

Gumbiner: I can remember it very vividly. In 1977, FHP got caught in a star chamber when Senator [Samuel] Nunn, who was then a junior senator from Georgia, was very interested in making his mark. He set up a Senate hearing investigation with just himself and his aides regarding the California Medi-Cal problem (that's what they called it). At that time Governor [Ronald] Reagan had decided to put as much as possible of the California Medi-Cal--that's the health care for the poor--into managed care. FHP had cut the cloth on that and had provided and developed the first health plan for Medicaid back in about 1968 or 1969. According to the then-legislative analyst, [A.] Alan Post, we were providing care [that was] as good if not better than the fee-for-service sector, and for about 25 percent less.

The mistake Governor Reagan made is a mistake that also could be made by the federal government in pushing all of Medicare into managed care. At that time, in his eagerness to save the state money and to control the costs in the provision of care, he gave contracts to everybody who applied. Some of these folks, either intentionally or unintentionally, took contracts and enrolled people that they couldn't supply the care for. So the people just didn't get the care, and it became a debacle. The result of all of that was that we all got tarred by the same brush.

FHP was known as the state of California's premier program. The secretary of health at that time--I can't remember his name, but he was voted as the most incompetent secretary of health in California history--simply canceled all of the contracts for every health plan in response to federal criticism.

The trade association, Group Health Association of America [GHAA], when I asked them what was going on and what should I do about testifying, responded, "Oh, we know you're a good guy. Just go in and tell the truth." Well, that turned out to be bad advice, because fundamentally, this investigation was a star chamber, a la Joe McCarthy: they were not interested in the truth, but were interested in publicity for Mr. Nunn and something dramatic. They were trying to prove that everybody involved was a crook. As a result of this, we lost our medical contract and about 50 percent of our income over a weekend.

Incidentally, we had the state of California coming around six months later asking us to take the contract back again. I was impressed that time by the fact that I couldn't depend on the trade association or anybody else to give me reasonable advice on what I should do, and [decided] that I would have to have my own legislative office.

Kaiser Permanente had a similar Medi-Cal/Medicaid program. They were not included in that investigation, because they had a Washington office. Their legislative office had called me and warned me about that a year or two ahead of time. Their lobbyist had been working diligently to get Kaiser Permanente exculpated, and he did. They were not even mentioned.

Hughes: So that was your impetus to establish a Washington office?

Gumbiner: Yes, a good lesson. It's like an insurance policy. You buy an insurance policy to insure your house from burning down, but probably in your lifetime your house never does burn down. But that doesn't mean you cancel your fire insurance. The people now in control of FHP have canceled that Washington office. They just don't understand that. They closed that office when we had probably the best legislative person in Washington working for us.

Hughes: This was right after the takeover?

Gumbiner: It didn't take them long--three or four weeks. They closed up the Washington and the Sacramento offices.

Hughes: Amazing strategy.

Gumbiner: So I don't know why they just don't cancel all of their insurance, because that was the same concept. But they are insurance people, so they have insurance-type brains. They don't understand that they can be hit with very difficult problems on the legislative front and they are absolutely helpless without coverage there.

Hughes: Don't they look around and see what other health plans are doing?

Gumbiner: Well, strangely, as far as I know, in Washington, D.C., the only HMOs that have legislative offices now are Kaiser Permanente--they have three or four people--HIP [Health Insurance Plan] of New York has a person, and I believe two or three others have contract lobbyists, which is not the same. Contract lobbyists will do what you tell them to do and that's about all they will do, because they are trying to serve several masters simultaneously.

Hughes: So they don't take any initiative?

Gumbiner: They are not your person. With your own lobbyist-and I usually don't call them lobbyists because that really has a different connotation; it's really a legislative office--they are watchful for all of your interests on the legislative front. They also do a constant educational program for the legislators and their staff. Your own legislative office is focused on your organization's interests and problems and have responsibility only for you.

The American Hospital Association [AHA] has about twenty lobbyists. The American Medical Association [AMA] has a number of lobbyists.

Hughes: Obviously this is part of the general cost-cutting moves in the health care industry, but is it also leading to something else that you were saying, namely, that a different breed of person has moved in? These people are interested in serving their investors, and they don't have a broad perspective that sees that health care involves people at all levels of society.

Gumbiner: You are right but it is part of a general naiveté. If you think about it, there are probably 200 to up to 300 HMOs in this country. And if you think about the fact that there are less than a half a dozen that have Washington offices, you come to the conclusion that these people are fairly naive about how our political system works.

Hughes: Has that always been true?

Gumbiner: It's always been true. They think that perhaps, in some way, the trade association is going to lobby for them, which of course doesn't always happen because the trade association also has several masters, and they may or may not be that effective. There is a general low level of management foresight in the conceptual or broader picture since the HMOs or the health care field are intimately involved in the federal and state governments' attitudes on health care. This should be a major HMO function.

Single-Payor Health Care

Hughes: You talked about your idea of the expansion of Medicare as a model for health care reform. Yet another idea that has been proposed for health care reform is the single-payor model, the Canadian model, where people have a card that they present to their doctor who submits a bill to some central government organization.

Gumbiner: I think the single payor was a red herring that was dragged across the path by the people that oppose reform. Because any way you turn, the federal government is the single payor of Medicare whether the federal government reimburses the insurance companies or the individual. I think that a better explanation of that is, the government as a direct payor versus the government as an indirect payor. Social Security does collect money from you out of your paycheck, and they do disburse the money. Whether they disburse the money through insurance companies or through HMOs or directly to the provider is the question.

Under Medicare today, they do both. In other words, they disburse the money to the doctor or patient, but they disburse it through fiscal intermediaries, for instance Blue Cross and some of the big insurance companies have contracts with Medicare but only process the claims. So fundamentally, the government is disbursing it directly through a fiscal intermediary. The government doesn't actually process its own claims. They are paying HMOs. Under the HMO Act, the government pays a flat sum of a capitated amount--so much per head per month--and then the HMOs provide the care. There they are paying the provider group or the HMO who then pays the provider. In either system the government is the single payor--and that's the way it is today.

The difference between that and the Canadian system is that the Canadian system is not just one system; each one of the provinces has a different way of paying for care. There, the federal government disburses the money to the provinces, and the provinces each have a little different system of benefits and claims. But they do then disburse it directly to the provider of care, whether it be a doctor, a hospital, or other. Fundamentally, in the United States the federal government is the single payor. If the federal government had 70 or 80 percent of the total population under Medicare, they could decide as the payor to do it any way they wanted to do it and set the benefit levels and level of payment.

The Business of Health Care

Hughes: I am thinking about your role in health care over a period of time: the fact that you started out as a physician and ended up being a manager with a business approach. I think I don't have to look too far to read into your remarks this afternoon some problem with the investor approach to health care. And yet, you somehow managed to combine those two perspectives. FHP as an organization had to run efficiently along business lines, and yet you also had a more humanistic approach and philosophy, providing the best care for the least cost to a wide number of people. How could you succeed in doing that where others didn't?

Gumbiner: I don't think these goals are mutually exclusive. You can still be altruistic and have social consciousness and run a business. It's a little bizarre to me that people think that just because you are socially conscious, you can't run a business, and that if you run an organization effectively and efficiently, you have no social conscious or altruism. The Catholic church certainly is a well-run business, and they are supposed to be altruistic, and are, in a sense. Some universities, for instance, are run efficiently and still have education and research as a goal.   There are all kinds of examples. I don't think that organizational efficiency and effectiveness is limited to the for-profit sector.

Hughes: No, but what you were saying about recent trends is that it is sort of a unidimensional approach--that the business aspect has taken over the humanitarian.

Gumbiner: I didn't say the business aspect; I said the interest of the investor has been given more prominence than the interest of the consumer customer and the interest of the staff, which I think is wrong. Anybody that knows anything about management knows it's wrong, because unless your staff is with you and appreciates what you are doing and is singing from the same hymn book, you are not going to get any efficiency out of them. There is no way that you can intimidate people to make them work hard and effectively, no way!

Secondly, health care is like any other service industry. We are providing a service. We are not manufacturing a product. If you are in the service industry, you have to provide satisfactory service. If you are in the auto industry and you provide a product, i.e. a car, and it's not acceptable to the public, then you don't sell any cars. So, it's pretty simplistic.

The only way I can see that this investor-first interest or greedy "me-first" philosophy can succeed is if it is on a very short-term basis. On that basis, management tries to build as much profit into the organization as they can and then they sell it to somebody and bail out. Hopefully, they can hoodwink the people that they are selling it to not to recognize what problems short-sighted management with no backup or growth potential will create. Sometimes the investors don't care; they just want to buy into the industry--the HMO field, or an insurance company may want just to buy the number of enrollees. They really don't care whether the number of enrollees is being served very well, or if the price of the service is correct, or if what they are paying the staff or the providers is correct, all of which has an effect upon whether they are to fail or succeed.

Hughes: The bottom line is, if an organization doesn't provide good medical care and good service, that's going to be corrective in itself eventually.

Gumbiner: It may be corrective in the sense that the investors will eventually lose money but some will sell out, perhaps before problems surface, they hope.

I think that the investors in a public company should get a reasonable return. They don't all have to become multimillionaires, but should get a reasonable return on their investment. After all, who is invested in the public area? Pension plans and mutual funds owned by the average worker who also receives the medical care.

The market has changed dramatically in the last five, ten years. Ten years ago, you used to have a lot of what they called retail or individual investors. Now most of these people buy mutual funds, where many, many people have invested their savings into pension plans and including people with their 401(K)s. These are just average people. I am sure if you asked them, "Would you rather make your job secure and have your company be successful? Or make a couple percentage points more on your fund return?", I think they would tell you they would rather have a secure job and work for a successful company where they liked to work.

Management has taken poll after poll on what people value the most on the job. What they universally value most on the job is a good place to work. They want to feel good about going to work; they feel like they're achieving something and that they are providing a valuable service. They are not usually interested only in money as long as they earn what they consider reasonable; making money is down about third or fourth on things they want out of their career.

Hughes:　　And FHP was successful in providing that atmosphere?

Gumbiner:　Well, I think so. I don't know if my secretaries handed you that whole pile of letters I got after I left.10

Hughes:　　They did. I haven't had a chance to go through it yet.

Gumbiner:　Well, when you get a chance to look at it, you will see what's what. We were pretty successful in offering career opportunities and a good place to work. I had several different types of training programs for staff. My idea was to provide an opportunity for everybody to grow within the organization and really feel more fulfilled with the type of work they were doing.

Hughes: And that, again, was one of the programs that was cut?

Gumbiner: Yes, that was decimated immediately--the training programs, the management programs, and the MBA [master of business administration] internships. For instance, when this guy Anderson took over, he immediately cut my galleries out. He said, "We are not in the art business!" What he doesn't understand because he's so naive is that he is in the business of selling health plans, and the art galleries are part of that business. The art galleries are a tremendous public relations tool, and we got more good P.R. and advertising mileage out of those art galleries than you can ever get per dollar any place else. He didn't understand that. He is not a manager.

Hughes: Did you argue that point with him?

Gumbiner: I never got a chance to debate anything. I was displaced in a surprise attack. You have to realize that I was ill. I came out of surgery and two weeks later they called a special meeting and got rid of the Office of the President, which I had created to protect Bill [W. W.] Price because he couldn't handle the job. He thought I was trying to diminish him, but he was wrong. Some board members were calling for his ousting. I was too sick to attend the next board meeting. Then the meeting after that, they snuck up behind me. The board members didn't say, "Let's have a debate, a discussion about Mr. Anderson's theories on how to run this company and Dr. Gumbiner's theories." That didn't happen. It was all done behind the scenes. It was all signed, sealed, and delivered in a conspiracy.

When I walked into the meeting that day after [Mark] Hacken had quit a half an hour before the meeting, I didn't have the votes. I though I had the votes four to four, but behind my back [Joe] Prevratil had negotiated an arrangement with Hacken that in return for a half a million dollars of a so-called "termination settlement", he would resign from the board a half hour before the board meeting. It was all set up. If be had resigned two days before, I could have thought about it a little bit and aborted the takeover. The timing was not a coincidence.

So there was no debate on this. I am not quite sure if the board really knew at that time the extent that Anderson was going to destroy this company. I cannot believe that Price was stupid enough to want to vote himself out of a job. As for these other two FHP board members that turned on me, perhaps it was more jealousy, envy, and resentment that motivated them rather than a desire to totally decimate and destroy the company.

Hughes: Well, we can get into that in more detail a little bit later. Is there anything more you want to say on this broader front?

Gumbiner: When you asked me how health care has changed, it is very interesting. It hasn't dramatically changed yet. I just think there is a meaner, less benevolent, caring atmosphere that flows down from the present Congress into business. A lot of people in business, particularly in for-profit public companies, are controlled by financial types. They just don't understand management, don't understand anything humanistic, and are just waiting for the signal. The signal came from Washington, "Yes, you don't have to have any social consciousness. You don't have to care about your fellow man or your employees. You don't have to have any long-range vision. You just go for it, line your pockets at others' expense."

I was walking down the street the other day and I saw a T-shirt that said, "Greed is Good".

Hughes: That goes along with your Four Horsemen of the Apocalypse philosophy.

Gumbiner: The Four Horsemen--envy, jealousy, greed, and hate--will destroy any organization. But interestingly enough, no one ever talks about these emotions and they remain hidden. But those emotions do exist.

In any event, the present orientation towards greed is a national catastrophe, as far as I can see. The feeling is, it's okay to be greedy and it's okay to exploit your fellow man just to line your pockets. To me, there is something wrong with that, because it's all right to be ambitious and try to make a living and do better financially. But when you are so wealthy that you don't need any more money, and yet you decimate an organization or wreck a whole concept and people's careers just to make some more money, it's bizarre.

Hughes: Well, even if you needed money, I think it's not exactly laudable. Presumably, a health organization--and I know you set up FHP not strictly as a money-making organization--provides a service for society.

Gumbiner: You are right; we were not running a discretionary service like a hotel or a restaurant. You don't necessarily have to go out to dinner that day; you can cook yourself some bacon and eggs at home. You don't have to go to a hotel; you can go to a motel or stay home. But if your child has a 104-degree temperature or you have a severe chest pain, you have to see somebody about it. Therein lies the whole problem, because the individual really does not have any choice. If you wanted to go to a hotel, you could go to a low-cost motel or to a very expensive five-star hotel; you have a choice. When you go out to a restaurant, you can get probably just as many calories by going to a fast-food place as you can by going to a fine dining place. But you have your choice. In products, you have your choice of what type of television or automobile you want to buy.

You don't have that choice in health care delivery. You don't know what it costs. And even if you know what it costs, you don't know if that is an appropriate cost or service. It is difficult to evaluate the provider care that you get. So it's a totally different situation. Health care is not really subject to market forces. The market theory dictates that the individual, the purchaser, can make a selection depending upon the quality versus the cost, if they wish. That does not usually occur in health care.

Now, with the HMO prepayment concept, the market concept gets closer because before you get sick, you can decide which HMO and benefits you want to buy. But on the other hand, some of the other elements still are there. It's hard to differentiate between HMOs since a lot of HMOs are turning out to be nothing but brokerage companies. They make an agreement or contract with the provider, doctor, or hospital on one hand, and on the other hand they make an agreement with the consumer. Usually it's the employer organization that pays for it, and subsequently the employee through payroll deduction or less payment. These HMOs are doing nothing new but just replicating and continuing the old fee-for-service system.

This system changes in the staff model HMO, where the organization hires the doctors, pays them a salary, and then charges a flat amount per month to the consumer. There are many examples of this system, such as the military. Most of our congressmen go to a staff model HMO. They either go to the Walter Reed Army Hospital or the Bethesda Navy Hospital and/or the medical schools.

Medical schools are another example of staff models. They hire the faculty who work for the medical school on a salary and have the professors take care of the patients. So there are several examples of staff model HMOs.

Until we get rid of the fee-for-service system, we are not going to get away from the problem of obtaining satisfactory health care for a reasonable cost.

That's what FHP has turned into now, simply a brokerage company. They are getting rid of their staff models and their hospitals and they are turning into a brokerage company that is simply arranging contracts in an attempt to put off the risk of the provider. But that doesn't work very well because you can't control the quality and availability of care through these contracts.

HMOs: For-Profit versus Nonprofit

Hughes: What about the trend within the HMO community towards for-profit rather than the original nonprofit organizations? How does that affect this trend that we are talking about?

Gumbiner: I think that is a key question. What has happened with our FHP HMO is that we worked as a not-for-profit for twenty years. Then it became obvious to me that two things were happening. First, since we are mostly a staff model and needed funds to expand, we couldn't get funding through conventional loans because there wasn't anybody to co-sign or stand behind an unsecured loan. Secondly, we were losing a lot of our good management people to for-profit organizations who were offering stock options, stock grants, and other marketing incentives.

So it seemed to me that we had to move to a for-profit format in order to generate the capital that we needed and attract personnel with stock options. If I remember correctly, initially this was simply a stock offering to raise money to pay for our first hospital. It took me three or four years to get that hospital financed. I finally had to go through the California Health Facilities Act for a loan, and that wasn't easy. So I said that if I have to do that forever, I will have a long grey beard before I get much done around here. That was pretty significant to me. The first public stock offering we mounted was to raise enough money to retire that loan, so we now owned our own hospital. That was pretty simple. We just sold part of the company stock and retired the loan. Now we didn't have to pay any debt service on the hospital; we were relieved of that expense.

Fundamentally, what we were doing was selling our company piecemeal through stock offerings. When we first started, I owned half the shares and the other managers owned the other half of the shares--simple. But in order to raise money, we had to start selling shares. So even if management hadn't sold any of their personal shares, we would have had to create more stock for sale, causing dilution. We converted and sold company stock to build the buildings and buy equipment. We ended up with the company more than half owned by investors as we expanded the number of shares and sold them. So we sold our company bit by bit.

Interestingly enough, the man that took over the company, this guy Anderson, only owns about 2.5 percent of the common stock. I think if you put everything together, common and preferred, he probably owns about 5 percent. That isn't enough to directly take over a company. So it's interesting that people can get in control through the back door with a reasonably small amount of stock. If it's a frontal takeover, then they have to buy a majority of the interest, over 50 percent, so they can control over 50 percent of the board of directors.

Hughes: What is a back-door takeover?

Gumbiner: A back-door takeover is where an individual or a group gets control of the board without buying a controlling interest in the stock and electing their slate of controlling board members. This guy Anderson has done this at least once before,

I understand. I will get into his history later. In a back-door takeover, in some way they either buy off the board members using company money or favors or discredit the present concepts and leadership one way or the other, and simply get control of the company through the board of directors. You don't have to own the company to get control of the company. You just have to have the votes on the board. So, that's the other takeover scheme.

Hughes: Was Anderson gambling, or did he have some assurance of some kind in advance?

Gumbiner: I really don't know. He received a premium for his stock in Takecare, part of which was in preferred stock for which he was getting a dividend. He also had common stock. His only gamble was that the company would not do well and his stock would go down in price. The other side of his game was to get control of FHP, liquidate it, sell the parts for more than the value of the whole, using the return on the sales to cover operating losses and to make it seem more profitable, pushing the stock price up and thus package it for sale at the highest price. When it's packaged for sale, then his stock price goes up, and he would make more money when the stock was sold. So he had nothing to lose if he didn't get control. He would just sit there and could eventually sell his stock. So he had little downside risk, only upside [possibilities].

How he managed to influence two of our board members is still a mystery to me, but we will get into it. I can tell you step by step how I perceived it was done.

You can control a company with a very small amount of stock. What's happening in American business today is that many of the founders may have a concept that made a company great but they moved out of the way either through death, retirement, or burden. Then other people come in who have different concepts and whose objectives are not to develop the founder's or the company's concepts but to do it their way for ego or material reasons. For some new people, if they are creative and achievement-oriented and want the company to grow, that's fine. It may just grow in a different direction.

Take Disney, for example. The company is now far from the concept of Walt Disney, but nevertheless they have a concept of a company which is growing and expanding and doing well. That's one situation which no one can argue with. On the other hand, if they are just there to destroy the company, to line their pockets, that's immoral and you can argue with that.

Some takeover artists, like Ross Perot, engaged in green mail. The company fundamentally bought him out just to get him off their board of directors. In other words, he got into these companies and caused them so much trouble and was such a threat to them that they bought him out. They paid him more for his stock than it was worth, just to get rid of him.

I think that any company that is buying a company should think about the major shareholder or board member that they are getting with the deal. If they are going to get a disruptive person or a predator, they should kill the deal right there because they are going to be in trouble. I may have been a little grandiose myself in thinking I could control Anderson and thinking that the board members were all on my side. It's a mistake not to have an investigating firm do a formal report on the people you are adding to your board of directors through the acquisition.

When a company gets to be well known, well financed, very progressive, with a lot of real estate and cash, it makes it a target for a predator to try to get hold of. They sell off the real estate, they grab the money; they dismember the company and use that to push up the stock price and line their pockets.

We knew that we were a prime target for a frontal takeover and prepared for it, but I just didn't conceive how a back-door takeover could work, that the management would collapse, and that the board members would betray the concepts that had built the company. But, being a student of human nature, I should have figured that out.

Hughes: Let me ask you just one, perhaps offensive, question. That is, business is like anything else; there are periods of development. Could some of this debacle be due to the fact that your idea of the staff model was passe?

Gumbiner: Well, that's what they tried to imply, that I was stuck with the staff model, but that was far from true. I had already converted FHP to almost 60 to 70 percent IPA [individual practice association--contracts with local doctors and hospitals for health care]. I saw the writing on the wall. I was always somewhat ahead of the field. My theory was a combined staff and IPA. I talked about that in the first oral history.

To me, a pure IPA model is very, very risky. All you have to do is lose the doctors' contracts and you are through, or the hospitals fill up and decide to raise their rates and you can't survive. The staff model combined with the IPA is much more secure, because that gives the HMO the capacity to either use or buy another hospital in an area if necessary, or to put staff models in amongst the IPAs, which we did in Arizona, where there were not enough doctors in certain areas of Phoenix. We had to keep developing staff models to support the IPAs which, to me, is the only way to make it work. I used a staff model merely to keep the company secure and going forward. That also set the tone for the quality of care. We can have better quality with our own facilities; we can pick and choose our doctors, and we control the availability. This sets the standard for the rest of the community and they have to keep up to compete.

When we went into Guam, we converted the whole island from a place where you couldn't find doctors on Wednesdays or the weekend or after five o'clock to a place where you could get care twenty-four hours a day.[11] Our centers were open twelve hours a day, seven days a week. When the rest of the doctors began losing their patients to us, they turned around and learned some different manners at the health care table. The combined model ensures quality of care and growth and vitality of the organization.

I even had a vision to acquire a prefab modular company and build an inventory of health-care centers so I would have them immediately available to be placed in needed locations. But all this stuff is visionary and designed for long-range success. You don't make as much money on the bottom line because you are engaged in research, training, recruiting, and preparing for future growth. If you are building for the next ten years and you buy a pre-manufactured modular manufacturing company to provide facilities for the next ten years, that costs money. But that assures that you are going to be available to provide the care, rather than scurrying around in an IPA and trying to make a contract with an orthopedist when there are only three orthopedists in the area and none of them want a contract. The solution is to bring two orthopedists into a staff model that is right in the middle of that IPA, and then they are not so busy any more.

I developed the combined staff and IPA [model]. It was predominantly IPA but controlled by the staff model. I also developed the FHP matrix management system, where the corporate entity controlled all of the different regions and there was a corporate overlay that made sure that the marketing and the recruiting were done the same way. It was like any good far flung organization, similar to a hotel chain like the Hilton, where all are units run on standards.

Hughes: Doesn't a staff model add to the overall HMO costs?

Gumbiner: Yes, but it is an investment in the future and in security and stability, a type of insurance well worth the cost. In my view, we cannot have health care reform without reforming the delivery system, and that means getting rid of all forms of fee-for-service and controlling the quality, availability, and access. The staff model does this.

Hughes: How does the staff model control an IPA?

Gumbiner: It's very simple. If the IPA doctors don't cooperate or they are not available, we can put a staff model unit in there to serve the consumers and eliminate them or increase the capacity.

Hughes: And they know that?

Gumbiner: That's right.

Managed Care, and More Changes in the Health Care Industry

Hughes: We have talked in general about health-care reform and related issues. I would like you to summarize by drawing the connections between the story we are about to tell of the FHP takeover and some of the themes that we were discussing earlier.

Gumbiner: What themes in particular would you like to discuss?

Hughes: We were talking about the possible discrepancy between the delivery of health care and investors' return, the consolidation of health plans, what the government is attempting to do with Medicare/Medicaid reform, and managed care as a solution to health-care delivery.

Gumbiner: These are slightly unrelated topics. Taking the consolidation of health-care programs: the consolidation of hospital chains and medical groups has been attempted for years. There is one theory that large, consolidated organizations that are nationwide work better. Unfortunately, it doesn't work quite that way in health care, because there are idiosyncrasies in certain geographic areas, particularly in the number of physicians, the type and number of specialties available, the general concept of how medicine is practiced, the delivery strategy, and the sophistication of the consumer. These idiosyncrasies cause a number of problems.

I don't know if consolidation as a strategy will ever be successful. Obviously, it is easier to run a larger organization than it is to run a smaller organization because you have a lot more backup and you can survive a lot more ups and downs. What was the first topic?

Hughes: The possible discrepancy between investors1 return and the delivery of good medicine.

Gumbiner: Right. But this conflict between corporate success, quality, and investors' return is not really related just to health care. The fact that U.S. management has lagged behind European and Japanese management due to its concentration on short-term profits and lack of long-term vision has been a lament of people that are sophisticated in management theory. The two—quality and investment return are antithetical, because in order to generate short-term profits, the company cannot put money into research and development, new long-range concepts, management training, and all the things that will build a long-term successful organization. So people who strictly have investors' return as their motive are not interested in long-term corporate guarantees.

As I mentioned before, the majority of investments are now being made by fund managers who either manage mutual funds or pension funds. Their personal income and their bonuses each year are based upon how they do for that particular account per year. So, obviously, if they have a stock that is doing well, they will sell it in order to realize a profit at the end of the year. If the stock is doing poorly, they will sell it in order to get it off their books. Along the same line, they are mainly interested in what quarter-to-quarter earnings are.

That really feeds into the other part of that problem.

That is, as any organization gets bigger, its percentage of growth in earnings has to be less, because it is a perfectly logical situation. If you have a company--just to pick a figure--that was making $100 million and it grew 20 percent, then it would grow $20 million in gross revenue. On the other hand, if a company was doing $1 billion, then it would have to grow $200 million in order to grow 20 percent. So as companies get bigger, their ability to maintain the same percentage growth is decreased because we are talking about bigger numbers, plus the fact that they are penetrating a finite market more deeply.

Finally, you just plain run out of customers. In other words, if you have 1 million people in your market and you have penetrated 20 percent, then you have 200,000 people available in that market. If you penetrated up to 50 percent, you would have 500,000 people in the market. There is going to be a certain number of people in that market that are not going to go into your HMO, either because they don't have insurance, they don't work, or they are on another program, and you just run out of market. Therefore, eventually, if you follow that line of development, the short-term investors would simply stop investing in this industry.

When you reach a certain level of market penetration the industry can't grow at the same rate, and the investors will go into the electronics industry, or something similarly innovative, where they can get that 100 percent or 50 percent growth, or whatever it is, pretty rapidly. That is a long explanation of a short question.

Your last question, managed care as a solution, relates directly to Medicare; most of the general population will be covered for health care by Medicare as the over 65 sector grows larger. The federal government, in regard to increasing Medicare costs, is faced with either raising the income, i.e. payroll withholding (unpopular), decreasing benefits (impossible), or eliminating the 30 percent waste and 20 percent fraud which can only be done through managed care. But that means less money for the providers and more political resistance from them.

FHP Under Bill Price

Hughes: My next thought was to talk about some of the changes in FHP under Price that had significance for the takeover. You are sighing.

Gumbiner: I retired in 1990, and I thought that I could retire as CEO and stop putting in my twelve hours a day, avoid the stress, and just be chairman. I would run the board of directors' meeting every quarter, and I would simply audit the agenda and take life easy. I would be there as an information and consulting resource for the management. They would consult with me and continue along the course that we had set. Price had been my number-two man for ten years, and for ten years he had appeared to agree with me on what we were doing. I thought that he would continue in the direction of long-range development of management backup, matrix support, innovative expansion, and independence and quality with the integrated staff model and IPA.

Hughes: Isn't that a usual course of action when a CEO retires? I mean, a chairman is not normally expected to run the company.

Gumbiner: Exactly. Unfortunately, Mr. Anderson is running the company as chairman. Anyway, what I had in mind was a traditional chairman's role.

Hughes: The one that you chose, not Anderson's?

Gumbiner: Yes. A chairman can be anything. Some chairmen micro-manage the company; they have the board behind them. They have what you call an "amen" board--whatever they say, the board says "amen". The chairman, in a sense, is the CEO. He can call the board together at a special meeting any time and fire the CEO.

Hughes: Does that work if the chairman is an adept person?

Gumbiner: I don't see how it can work, and I will tell you why. The chairman can't get enough information to make educated decisions unless he or she puts in the time to talk to the people, visit the sites, read the reports, go to the meetings, and do all the things you have to do to get information. The CEO's job is essentially one of gathering enough information upon which to make decisions. If the chairman is not available a significant amount of time, he can't get the information. It is different in the case of Anderson; he is simply dismantling and liquidating the company. There are no problems of creating--just orders to sell and fire.

Price, unfortunately, seemed to take the advice of the last person he talked to. He had a COO [chief operations officer] that was aggressive and definitely pushed his ideas, and Price seemed to go that way. So the first thing that happened was that Price canceled the matrix management. I called him and asked him why he had canceled the matrix management. We had spent years developing that. The reason we had worked on it and developed it was because of the type of organization we had; it was spread out geographically, managed a lot of knowledge workers, and was a complicated service. It was part financial risk projection, part insurance company, part health care delivery, part a medical group, and part a lot of different things.

Price tried to lie to me and tell me we still had the matrix, when in fact we didn't have the matrix.

Hughes: How could he lie about that? Either the company did or didn't.

Gumbiner: Well, he would say, "We still have it in part." What he did was take out certain sections, or he kept the corporate functional portions but didn't give them power to manage in the regions; just oversight.

Hughes: Under what principle?

Gumbiner: He had this notion that if you decentralize things, they would work better because the people in the decentralized areas knew more about the local conditions than the corporate executives did. That is exactly the opposite philosophy from matrix because, in my thinking, you would have to have ten or twelve really competent, multi-talented CEOs, one in each region, to do that. They would have to know a lot about marketing, about health care delivery, about finance and many of the other different fields.

The probability of getting these dozen top executives all running these divisions is very low, because the divisions really weren't that big. In addition, you would lose the advantage of scale and standardization plus specialized support.

So in the matrix system, you found your best person in marketing who was a specialist in that, your best person in finance who was your chief financial officer, your best person in health-care delivery, and so forth. These specialists then controlled their areas in the regions along with their regional manager. They were experts, and the regional manager would operate and make all these things happen. They were broad gauged specialists in coordination and delivery.

Hughes: So what happened under Price's system was that the regional managers then had to have a variety of expertise?

Gumbiner: Correct. This was not an unusual direction for a person like Price, who didn't have the ability to run the organization. He felt that by redirecting the responsibility to the regional managers, he would avoid personal responsibility in the central organization. In other words, if Arizona's marketing was weak, then it wasn't his problem because he didn't have a corporate marketing division. It was the Arizona manager's responsibility that the region's marketing was weak. That made life easy for Price.

Now, we see a bit of that in the federal government trying to refer block grants to the state governors. In that situation, if there is a block grant for Medicaid, care for the poor, it is deferred to a state governor. He is supposed to take the block grant, distribute the money, and take care of the poor. If he or she doesn't, it is really not the federal government's problem; it is that particular governor's problem.

Of course, anybody who thinks about it knows that it doesn't work, because you would have to have fifty governors, all fully competent, doing all these great innovative things and taking care of the poor.

So the heart of any company is it has a direction, a mission, a focus, and a policy. That policy goes throughout the company. You wouldn't have each Hilton hotel manager running the hotel the way he wanted to run it, or each McDonald's hamburger manager running things his way, and so on.

Hughes: We are naming Price, but in actual fact, wasn't [Mark] Hacken also part of this?

Gumbiner: In the beginning, there was a man named Pat Vitacolonna, who was the COO, who was pushing Price to change things. Pat was a very energetic, innovative guy, but, in my view, his judgment wasn't very good. One time, I came in to find that he had convinced Price to raise the surcharge on our prescription drugs in the Medicare program from three dollars per prescription drug to seven dollars. You can't raise the prescription drug surcharge threefold. You could possibly raise it from three dollars to four dollars, or maybe five dollars, but certainly not to seven. That is the bean counter's mentality, to take the number of prescriptions, multiply them by seven dollars, and voila, you have cured your financial problem, because now for every one of those prescriptions you are getting seven dollars, not three.

Except for one problem: you are probably going to get half the prescriptions filled, because these people are going to quit the program, or they are not going to buy the prescriptions. It destroys the very concept of a program in which prescription drugs are available at a very low cost so that people get them and use them and get well. If they have to pay seven dollars, they might not fill their prescriptions. When they don't, they get sicker, the hospital bills are higher, or they quit the program altogether.

Pat Vitacolonna was also great at putting a limit on the pharmacy program because he was previously a pharmacist. That again doesn't work, because if the concept is that you have your prescription drugs available for a patient stop-loss of three dollars a prescription, people will pick up the prescription drugs and take them and won't end up in a more expensive hospital bed. What is the difference in achieving this objective if you have a $600 cap and reach the $600, and now they have to pay full bore, so they don't get their prescriptions and they end up in the hospital?

Vitacolonna's concept was that that [policy] would get rid of people who were big users. In other words, people would know that they only had $600 worth of prescription drugs, and they would go join another program and quit our program. That didn't make a whole lot of sense to me anyhow, because people never kept track of when they were going to reach their $600. So all of a sudden, bingo, they didn't have prescription drugs covered, so they didn't get them; they didn't take them, and they ended up in the hospital. They knew they could get the drugs in the hospital if they were an inpatient. "Well, Doctor, I may die of a heart attack because I can't buy the medication I need, but if you put me in the hospital, I will be all right. On the way out, I will get my prescriptions filled."

Price went through all these different gimmicks. He went for a packaged quality control program gimmick when actually quality control is the concern of any good management group, not just some gimmick where somebody comes in and trains your people and leaves. The only people that make any money out of these quality control schemes are the people that put them together and sell them to other people.

Hughes: What was Price's quality control scheme?

Gumbiner: It was a scheme that was conceived by an individual. He sold it as a package and came in and trained people in quality control. The concept was that each person had responsibility for quality. Nothing revolutionary.

Hughes: What had FHP been doing in terms of quality control?

Gumbiner: We had quality control programs going. The doctors, the nurses, and other sectors all had the concept--it was part of the overall strategy--but first one must define quality.

Hughes: What was the difference?

Gumbiner: The difference was that now Price didn't have to worry about it or be responsible because he had this head of quality control that had this packaged, pre-masticated, pre-digested concept. All the outside organization had to do was set up the program and train the employees, and now the people do all the good things they are supposed to do. Which, of course, doesn't work, because you constantly have to reinforce it. It involves recruiting the right people because there are people that, no matter how much training you give them, they don't do it. Besides, Price no longer had these responsibilities.

Hughes: These were people hired just to do quality control?

Gumbiner: Right.

Hughes: But before, it had been up to the people actually doing the work to maintain quality?

Gumbiner: It was up to the people; it was part of their job. Just like teaching a class. When you teach a class, say you have twelve students. Some get A's, some B's, some C's, some D's, and some F's. Why is that? They all heard the same lecture. Well, because some are smarter than others, some care more than others, some concentrate, some pay attention.

There is no gimmick that is going to do quality control. It is the whole series of systems with constant reinforcement, getting rid of the people that can't do it, hiring people that can. The heart of quality control is the right people. You can't make a silk purse out of a sow's ear.

Hughes: We are talking about changes that played into the eventual takeover, and decentralization seems to be a theme. Were there other things that were being done to change the philosophy behind FHP?

Gumbiner: For one, they began selling IPAs in the staff model catchment area, which was a mistake. I told them that was a mistake in the beginning and that they were cannibalizing their own organization. In the staff model catchment area, you have the staff model medical group and a hospital limited to a certain geographic area for enrollees. Usually about a twenty-minute drive to a medical center and probably about an hour drive to a hospital is acceptable.

They had the notion that if we didn't put together IPAs in these catchment areas, in what they call overlay on the staff model, that other HMOs would come in there and take those customers. I didn't believe that because, sure, other IPAs may have taken some of the consumers, but we were giving away 100 percent of the opportunity for our staff models. If the staff models were competing against the IPA HMOs, they might get 50 percent of the consumers and the HMOs would get 50 percent.

So obviously what happened was it was a lot easier for the salesmen to sell an IPA. "Oh, would you like to have a doctor in your backyard?" "Who is your doctor? We'll make a contract with that doctor." As an alternative for the staff model they would have to sell the concept of one-stop health care and everything in one place in the staff model, perhaps a new concept. They lost sight of the fact that the fee-for-service community was the enemy of the staff model and the competitor and they were not our friends.

That was a big mistake, and obviously that led to the fact that the staff model didn't grow that fast and well as it should have.

The staff model is one concept, the IPA is another concept, and you don't sell both of them in the same place. My concept of having the staff models and their catchment area surrounded by the IPAs outside the catchment area was a workable theory. An alternative idea was a combined staff model and IPA, as we had in Arizona and New Mexico, where we put in the IPAs and we plugged in the staff models, which were just medical centers and doctors in the places where we didn't have IPA doctors.

Hughes: Where you didn't have IPAs?

Gumbiner: Yes, where the doctors didn't exist. In the south part of Phoenix there is a big housing development, and there are only five doctors there. Obviously, these people were as busy as they could be and weren't interested in cooperating with anybody, so there weren't any available doctors [for an IPA]. We put a ten-doctor staff model in there. One of the failings of the IPA is that you can only deal with the doctors that exist there. You really can't develop a health-care delivery system, because if you only have two orthopedic surgeons and you really need five orthopedic surgeons, then you can't get adequate orthopedic services.

What you do then in the combined program is you put three orthopedic surgeons into your staff model, so you can actually fill in for the service that you lack from the IPA.

Hughes: In general, the control over an IPA is minimal compared to a staff model?

Gumbiner: Absolutely. Number one, you can't require doctors in an IPA to work at a particular time. If it is the habit in the community for all the doctors to play golf on Wednesday afternoon and not to be in their office on Saturday and Sunday, too bad; you can't find a doctor. You have to go to the emergency room and find a doctor who may not speak English.

Hughes: So, in a sense, you have to take what you can get.

Gumbiner: Exactly. You take what you can get in quality, availability, and accessibility. Doctors are like anybody else. Some are lazy, some are diligent, and so forth.

Hughes: Do you think that is going to change with this new picture that is emerging in health care? The physicians, even in what might be loosely phrased as an IPA, are going to have to kowtow to more guidelines about medical practice. And if so, how would that control be exerted?

Gumbiner: If you control their pocketbooks, their hearts and minds will follow.

Hughes: That's very "Gumbinerian"!

Gumbiner: Fortunately, money is not the ultimate motivation, but it can be a preventer or persuader. We all know about sales organizations in which you may have ten salesmen of which two salesmen are selling 80 percent of the product or service. Yet, what happened to the other eight salesmen on the same commission basis, who are not making a very good living? They are either

43

lazy, incompetent salesmen, they don't like sales, or one thing or another.

You have the same thing in doctors. At least in doctors there is a baseline--people that have gotten through medical school are mostly hard-working and smart enough to have done so. On the other hand, what happens to them ten years out is something else again. Some people may not want to work that hard any more. They have expectations, and they may have what I call the "entitlement theory". After they go through medical school, they are entitled to make a good living with minimal effort because they did all this hard work and have an M.D. degree.

I went to medical school with people whom the military sent to medical school, and they tried to tell me what income they were entitled to because they went to medical school with all that hard work and expense. Most of them went to medical school so that they wouldn't get shot at in World War 11 and they did not pay for it. Many doctors have the entitlement attitude; I'm not saying all of them.

I think that when there are more restraints on what they can do, some physicians will make less because they won't work any harder; they won't change their particular habits, because they can't. They are not going to change their attitude or their view of life. If money were the great motivator, then we would have no poor people. Everybody would get an education. They would work hard and deny immediate gratification for long term success. We would have no lower middle class. We would have nobody complaining about inadequate income, because everybody would work effectively for fifteen hours a day, six days a week.

So I think that money is not the great motivator. In all the studies we have done on our doctors and our managers, money is down there third or fourth as an objective to work for. Interestingly enough, money is lower on the scale of things doctors than it is with managers. For most people, in all the studies I've done and all I've seen, the main thing they want out of a job or career is a place in which they enjoy working, a feeling that they are contributing, and a sense of control over their own destiny. Money is down third or fourth, as long as it is adequate, except for the investors, the bean counters, who are in the game just for money. For some reason, to the materialistic mind, if they can own a bigger house, buy a bigger car, then that is a measure of their achievement in life.

In my view, accumulating money is not a measure of achievement. The materialistic person will never leave a mark on history or contribute to social welfare. That is the major difference, I think, with the people like Price and [Jack] Massimino who are managing FHP now. They have no achievement orientation whatsoever, other than making money for themselves. They also allow people on Wall Street to frighten them. People on Wall Street are so imbued with money-making, they lose sight of other more satisfying, more altruistic objectives. They will just work on anything that's easy to get. They lose their objectivity and any broad-range perspective. So, all they do is work in this money field day in and day out, and their goal is how much money they can make for themselves or their clients. They lose sight of the larger world.

Hughes: How has Wall Street gotten to Price and Massimino?

Gumbiner: These guys would go to the East Coast and make quarterly presentations to the financial analysts, fund managers and investors and agree with whatever the investment managers wanted. Whereas, if somebody on Wall Street said something to me after a presentation, I might say, "No, I don't agree with that. We are not going to do that." For example, if somebody said, "Why don't you generate more earnings per quarter?", I would say, "No, we are not generating more earnings per quarter because we are pumping our earnings into future development and long-term success by training people, developing new concepts, building for the future, and returning something to society. By investing in training consumers about nutrition and alternate lifestyles, such as stress management, we avoid problems and expensive medical care, but that does not immediately show up on the bottom line."

Hughes: Preventive medicine.

Gumbiner: Yes. The biggest part of preventive medicine is removing the barrier for the potential patient in receiving health care. The barrier is that they think it is going to cost them fifty, sixty, or a hundred dollars to visit the doctor. In the low income areas, they say, "If I go to the doctor, it is going to cost me fifty dollars. I want to be fifty-dollars sick." So they end up in the hospital because they cannot judge when they are 'fifty dollars sick'. But Wall Street could not conceive of investment to pay for long-term gain because it doesn't increase the price per share the next quarter.

For instance, if we were to develop a medical school within an HMO, using the HMO hospitals which are already there, we would not only cut the cloth for a better, more efficient type of medical school, curriculum-wise, but also economy-wise we would be able to attract a better mix of altruistic people by lowering the tuition or even paying people to go to medical school, which is not so bizarre. During World War 11, the U.S. government paid for all of us to go to medical school. We would avoid what we are going to have in the future, which is all upper-class white doctors. There are not many black or Latino doctors who can afford to go to medical school. We will end up with all upper-class white doctors.

But a medical school doesn't make any immediate money for the investors. You can imagine the public relations that such a merger would engender. You would raise your HMO to another level. You would be a medical school HMO, which would get rid of all this garbage about second-rate HMO doctors that they yap about, which is not true.

As I mentioned, when Anderson took over our company, the first thing he got rid of was the art galleries. He didn't understand. He said, "We are not in the art business." What he didn't understand was that we are in the business of marketing and enrolling people in the HMO, and the art galleries gave us lots of P.R. mileage, just like the medical school would have given us lots of mileage. But Wall Street doesn't think that way. So they intimidate our two FHP guys and say, "Why aren't you making more money this quarter? Why do you have these training programs? That doesn't make money." Everybody knows that training programs do make money down the road, but they don't make money the next quarter.

More on Nonprofit versus For-Profit Health Care

Hughes: How does the health-care system avoid control by Wall Street? It used to be that health care was dominated by nonprofit organizations, nonprofit health plans.

Gumbiner: Not exactly, because all the big medical groups are for-profit. The doctors are for-profit. Let's face it. I know very few doctors that are nonprofit, that will work for nothing. A few maybe work for Doctors Without Borders or something like that. But in general, there is a difference in working to make a living and working just to pile more dollars on top of dollars.

Hughes: I was thinking in the organizational sense. If you have a nonprofit organization, you are less likely to give credibility to anything that an investment manager is going to tell you. You have no reason to.

Gumbiner: I don't think that is the answer, because not-for-profits will never get big enough to move fast enough to do what they have to do, development-wise or competitively, because they don't have the financing.

Hughes: Kaiser is a nonprofit.

Gumbiner: Kaiser is not doing well right now.

Hughes: Because of changes in the health care market?

Gumbiner: Yes. They decided they were being beat up by the IPAs. I talked to some of the Kaiser people who came down to talk to me about whether they should go the way that FHP went. I said, "No, you should not. You should just advertise and market better." That is the key. Nothing is ever bought; it's sold!

Hughes: You mean they were considering going to a for-profit model?

Gumbiner: No. They were considering getting rid of their hospitals. The Kaiser people are really not a great marketing operation. They were there first with a lot of money. Let's face it. When they started out, they didn't have any money. But guess what? Guess who signed all the notes? Henry J. Kaiser, who was for-profit. That is the way that Kaiser got their hospitals and their medical groups. Henry J. Kaiser co-signed their notes. Easy, right? Well, most not-for-profits don't have that advantage.

Hughes: But that is true of only the very beginning history of Kaiser Permanente. Surely, Henry J. can't be pointed to as the reason for Kaiser's later success.

Gumbiner: By the time Henry J. Kaiser was out of the picture, they had such a big mass of gross and net income that the mass was carrying them. Now they are having trouble growing against the competition. Market share is the problem; not a problem of survival.

Hughes: And you attribute Kaiser's growth problems to poor salesmanship and marketing?

Gumbiner: No. It's their not-for-profit attitude. They are not that vigorous in their marketing. Let's face it: they don't attract the real dynamic managers at the top. That was one reason that I went for-profit: I was losing my managers. Why would somebody break their back working for a not-for-profit when they could make several million dollars by doing the same amount of work in a for-profit?

Let me expand on this; it's contiguous. On one end, you have the not-for-profit HMOs which never have enough capital and can't attract really strong managers and move ahead dynamically. You usually attract people who like routine and want to avoid risk and don't want to be bothered with growing. Why would they? What is in it for them?

Then, you move on to the private for-profit HMOs—not public. Managers can achieve financial rewards there and don't have to worry about Wall Street. Wall Street and their misbegotten advice can be ignored, because in a private company the investors are usually also the management. But this type of structure is short on financing, which inhibits their growth.

Then, you move over to the public-offered for-profits which are more or less beholden to Wall Street, depending upon how much of the company was sold to investors. If only 25 percent was sold, they could thumb their noses at the investors. If they sold a lot of their company to the public but the management and the board was strong and philosophically together, they could say, "Fine, so what if our stock is languishing at twenty dollars a share and a competitor's is up to forty dollars a share? We are not playing in that ball game. Let others chase their tail and try to get to sixty dollars a share and suffer the risks, problems, and uncertainty of manipulating the stock price. We are here to deliver health care and for long-term growth and stability."

Hughes: And that would be a viable stance?

Gumbiner: That would be a viable stance. There is nothing Wall Street can do about it, and there are some who can understand this.

Hughes: How do you keep your investors?

Gumbiner: That doesn't bother me. There is always somebody who is going to invest in your long-term program. There is always somebody who is going to buy a twenty-dollar share when all the other shares are forty dollars, because it is less expensive and has more opportunity to go up, not down.

The problem is that it is harder to raise money. If you want to sell another quarter of a million shares of stock in a public offering and you can get sixty dollars a share, the company will get $60 million for a million shares. If, on the other hand, your stock is twenty dollars a share, you are going to get $20 million for a million shares, right? You are selling the same portion of your company but for a lot less. That would be the impinging problem. You have to sell a larger portion of your company to raise the same amount of money. But on the other hand, long-range, I think you would come out better.

It is just like the savings and loan industry. The savings and loans that were not running around in the 1980s making all these high-risk loans to developers didn't make a lot of money during those days. The savings and loans that were making all these strange loans to real estate developers for high rates made a lot of money short-range, but they went bankrupt eventually and were taken over. The question is, do you want to invest in an HMO that has a long-range strategy for success or one that has a short-range, high-risk strategy? Everybody knows this. There have been millions of things written about it. Wall Street is interested in short-range profits. They look at the stock market every day. Is the stock going up or down?

The Importance of Management with Vision

Hughes: So what you are saying is that the way that you ensure the delivery of top medicine and also avoid undue control by Wall Street is to have top managers and a knowledgeable board of directors?

Gumbiner: You have to have managers and a board of directors that are together, who know what the company wants to do and where it plans to be in the future. They must have a vision, have a strategy and the courage to stick to it. They cannot be distracted by the sniping of the thirty-two-year-old guys on Wall Street that are only interested in short-range profits, who never ran anything in their lives, and who are trying to give your managers and board of director's advice in their own self-interest.

Now, I never listened to them. As a matter of fact, I would lead them, not let them lead me. I would tell them what we were going to do, why we were going to do it, and what I expected to happen. You know, it's a sales deal. I've watched Price and Massimino perform and all they do is side-step and make excuses. You don't do that. You tell people what your vision is and you lead them through it and convince them of its validity.

For instance, back in the late 1980s, all the Wall Street gurus said that Medicare risk contracts were not the way to go for HMOs; you shouldn't have a Medicare risk program with the federal government.[12] I said you should have a Medicare program. I stood there and told them, "Look, federal Medicare risk contracts are the way to go." In the future there will be more older people. We started in 1966 with 13 million risk-contract older people covered under Social Security, and now we have 37 million in 1996. We are going to have 60 million older people in 2010. I didn't care that they kept telling me, "Everybody says that Medicare risk contracts are bad. All you do is lose money. All the other HMOs have lost money." Forget it. We made money on it; we did a good job for the beneficiaries.

Now, ten years later, it's all turned around. All of the HMOs and doctors want Medicare risk contracts. So make up your mind objectively; don't listen to Wall Street.

Hughes: But you had had years and years of experience in health care delivery, and the experience was with different models and different forms. Most people don't have that. The problem with your argument is that it is difficult to find people that combine vision plus actual experience in the health care field.

Gumbiner: It's hard to find people with vision. Price had ten years with me. For ten years he followed me around the political halls of Washington and New York's financial world. Why didn't he understand what was going on? Why in the end did he take the advice of people with less success and less experience? Because he had no courage or self-confidence.

Hughes: But he had the experience, you think?

Gumbiner: Yes. He was there for ten years, all through the 1980s.

Hughes: So you don't think it is impossible to find people that combine those two attributes?

Gumbiner: They are there. There are just not too many of them around. It is hard to find people with successful experience, vision, and courage of their convictions.

Hughes: According to you, what happened in the FHP takeover is that people who had those attributes were replaced by investors.

Gumbiner: Visionaries have a hard time hanging on unless they are very practical and they become Machiavellian. Sometimes you lose your base because you get so carried away with the vision that you forget to include the troops. It is like the lieutenant that jumps up and charges forward. He looks around and he doesn't have anybody with him. The guys are all hiding in the foxholes; they are not with him.

Hughes: Did you have that problem?

Gumbiner: Oh yes, always. I had to drag them out of the foxholes to come along.

Hughes: Were they in the foxholes because your eyes were off on the horizon?

Gumbiner: Yes. I would say categorically, I did not pay enough attention to massaging and orienting the board of directors. I don't think they had a clue of what I was doing or what I was thinking about.

Hughes: All the way through, you mean?

Gumbiner: The last few years. I would say probably the last three or four years. I was so busy with Price and Massimino; I think Massimino was the most difficult problem of all, because he was a very crafty and self-centered young man. He was the one that kept pushing Price to dismember the company, decentralize it, and change it. These people that don't have vision and don't have courage always take the easy way out. What is the easy way out? Give the responsibility to somebody else. Decentralize, reinvent--give the responsibility to someone else.

Hughes: What should you have been doing?

Gumbiner: What I should have been doing is formally, through special board meetings, and informally, through socializing, apprising the board members of the problems as I saw them and bringing them along through the same process I had gone through to reach the same conclusion, particularly in regard to management. The managers should have been continuing the matrix, or some form of it, and marketing, marketing, marketing. They should have been marketing the staff model. As consultant and chairman, I attempted several times to get the organization to go into manufacturing pre-manufactured modular medical centers so FHP could expand faster. But when I turned my back, they would be building a one-of-a-kind "stick model". Now, you have to realize that if you as chairman don't go to the office every day to maintain contact, and the only contact you have is once every couple of weeks or so, management may do things behind your back.

Anderson's management style is to terrorize management. He simply liquidates people and departments. That doesn't take much effort. He calls Price up two or three times a week and tells him to fire this or that person or, since he has the majority of the board of directors behind him, Price will be liquidated if he objects.

I don't know if you have ever seen the picture "Caligula". Caligula makes a great statement. He says, "I don't care if they love me, as long as they fear me." Caligula periodically took three or four senators and had them killed. People would say, "Those are good men." So what. He simply replied, "They were disloyal. I don't want them to love me; I want them to fear me." In the end, he was murdered by the captain of his guard.

So that is Anderson's theory: it works to terrorize. But the people who are left are only the frightened and incompetent.

Communicating with FHP's Board of Directors

Hughes: The other point you just made is that the chairman needs to keep his board up to date on his philosophy. You mean to say that you weren't doing that?

Gumbiner: No, I wasn't doing that.

Hughes: Why was that?

Gumbiner: Because I was really burned out or bored. For thirty years, I had been conducting four boards of directors meetings a year for FHP, four for the foundation, and committee meetings, and auditing, and reading minutes and reports. I resented going to another board meeting. It takes a couple of days just to go over the material to run a board meeting properly. You have to go over the financials and all the reports from management people and outsiders, as well as plan the agenda and review all board and committee reports. It's too much year after year.

Hughes: Were you doing that?

Gumbiner: Yes, I was doing that. I had to go over the agenda and make sure it was not too long, not too short, covered enough things.

   I had to make sure that the board members were on the right committees. I had to go to the committee meetings to see how they were doing. When you have about four or five committees and you have board meetings and they all meet quarterly, you are going to a number of meetings. Most of all, in chairing the meetings, it is necessary to concentrate on drawing certain people out and shutting others up, all without hurting their egos or creating implied or imagined slights.

Hughes: Were you doing any of that?

Gumbiner: I was doing that, and with preparation, reading all the material. The material the Audit and Finance Committee alone gave you was an inch and a half thick. I resented that. I had been doing it for years and years, and I didn't retire in 1990 to be that involved. I thought that I knew the board members well enough to relax and ignore the interpersonal relationships, but I think it takes constant effort. You have to have them in for dinner parties, socialize, do one-on-ones, pretend to seek their advice. You have to do all these different things.

If you find a board member that you don't have confidence in and who you think is not contributing, you should get rid of him or her, either get them to retire and put them on an advisory committee, or when the time comes up for their reelection, you should very carefully review a list of criteria and if they don't measure up, you should not re-nominate them. Otherwise they will sense that they are not respected and ally themselves with any faction that is out to get you, (i.e. Anderson). Over the years, people change personality-wise, financially, politically--a good argument for term limitations.

One of my big problems is I was always looking for the eminently successful, qualified board member. In particular, I was looking for board members who had worked as CEOs in the service industry and for big, successful companies. Those are hard to find. I didn't want people from the manufacturing industry because it is not the industry we are in. They don't understand what the service industry is. So I was searching for potential board members in the hotel industry, the restaurant industry, the airline industry, the amusement industry, all service industries. They were very hard to find. You would be amazed how many people I interviewed that were presidents of companies who were not acceptable. They didn't know management theory nor have a concept of organizational structure. They had no vision.

I talked to industry people after the takeover, and they said they couldn't figure out why Price was there so long. He was there so long because of my delinquency, because I didn't want to spend the effort to replace him and spend six months on a search. I was not focused.

Hughes: Also, you created the Office of the President, which presumably was at least partially designed to spread authority and remedy the situation. You essentially had two people instead of one.

Gumbiner: I created the Office of the President [October 1993) in order to help Price and to give more dimension and power to that office. He didn't understand that. Machiavelli says, "When you have an enemy, don't wound them, kill them." Price wasn't my enemy, but he became my enemy in his mind because he thought I was trying to diminish his authority. I had concluded that this job of running a big organization, in addition to expanding and growing, was too big a job for one person. Actually, I was trying to help him [by creating the Office of the President].

It was a serious mistake on my part to create the Office of the President. I should have grabbed the bull by the horns at that time and made a decision. What I was looking at was written evaluations of Price by all the board members, including my own evaluation, that didn't give Price a high enough evaluation to keep him. I was evaluating him at about

50 percent effectiveness. So I was faced with two possibilities: fire him or strengthen him.

Evaluating a CEO

Hughes: What sorts of things do you look at when you evaluate a CEO?

Gumbiner: I worked out a CEO evaluation form which contains things such as innovation, vision, communication, ability to prioritize, judgment, decisiveness, general management ability, achievement orientation, competence in various areas, political skills, broad-based knowledge on health care delivery, ability to focus on cost and quantity, presence and stature, honesty, humanistic character.

Hughes: All the board of directors used those criteria for evaluation?

Gumbiner: I was sitting on a hot potato, because it didn't appear to me that they thought that much of Price. Therefore, if based on the evaluations I had, he should have been removed. I would have had to go on a search and I didn't feel that there was that much talent on the outside. There were also a lot of different things that were happening in my private life. I was worried about my prostate cancer, I was getting married again, and I didn't really want to take the time and energy to attempt to find and orient another CEO at that time, and that was a mistake. Perhaps I couldn't believe that Price would not improve.

I would say, as advice to anybody that is chairman of a board, if you don't have confidence in your CEO, get an evaluation from all your outside board members and sit down with them. Go over the problems, and if he or she does not measure up in the collective board members' appraisal, then you have to terminate that person. Then you have to go out and look for somebody else and take your chances.

Hughes: So, in essence, your creation of the Office of the President was a stopgap measure?

Gumbiner: Correct. It was a temporary alternative. I thought that this fellow, Mark Hacken, who theoretically had put together the Thrifty Jr. chain, was strong enough and innovative enough to help Price focus and make decisions and make the Office of the President work. I thought that he agreed with my philosophy and would be an energetic surrogate for me. He told me that he was definitely in favor of centralization, not decentralization.

In reality, what happened was that Hacken wasn't strong enough, and this guy Massimino got together with Price and they rolled right over him. They lied to him. They would go to important meetings which they didn't tell him about, and they would keep information from him. They used every dirty trick they could think of to discredit him.

Hughes: Was Price from the start cognizant of the significance of what you were doing by creating this Office of the President?

Gumbiner: I thought he was, but in retrospect, he didn't want to understand it. I think his wife got on his case, too. She thought he was just wonderful. It was just one of those problems where you have a person that is just not up to the job. He would have made a good chief financial officer for a company someplace, or he might have made a reasonably good CEO for a small HMO, maybe in the nonprofit field. He had the ambition but not the ability. He was not decisive nor creative or courageous. They tried to unseat him about two years into his job.

Hughes: Who is "they"? The board?

Gumbiner: Pat Vitacolonna, the COO [chief operations officer], and certain members of the board tried to get rid of him. Their accusation was that he was indecisive, didn't know anything about the medical/HMO business. It wasn't the fact that he didn't know anything about the medical business; he just didn't know enough about management. But when somebody is your number-two person, it is easy for them to act like they know because they just say, "Yes, that's a good idea, fine." Then they carry things out.

Anyway, a lot of number-two people who get promoted to number one can't measure up to the ambiguities when they are sitting there alone and they have to make their own decisions. They don't have courage and they don't have decisiveness. They don't have focus, and then they can't do it. In Price's case, he leaned on his COO, who had his own agendas. So that was a mistake on my part.

I would say that unless the chairman pays attention to the board of directors and works with them constantly, the chairman will lose control, influence, and power. The chairman has to like and respect the board of directors. If there are people he doesn't like and doesn't respect, then he should get rid of those people, because they are not going to work well with him, and this comes out indirectly. Then these board members get resentful and look for ways to get rid of that chairman. They will line up with anybody.

There were certain Indian tribes that lined up with Cortez when he came in to Mexico because they hated the Aztecs. They were just looking for some way to get rid of the Aztecs. If it wasn't Cortez, it could have been any strong ally. I firmly believe that anybody could have done it. It didn't have to be Anderson. It is just too bad that it had to be a mercenary predator who wanted to wreck the company. If somebody like Anderson wanted to come in and build the company, these board members, I believe, would have gone over to him just because they felt neglected and not consulted.

II. THE MERGER OF FHP AND TAKECARE
The Concept of the TakeCare Acquisition

Hughes: Tell me how the acquisition of TakeCare came about? Whose idea was it?

Gumbiner: When I created the Office of the President [October 1993] that gave Price more time to do other things. He realized that he was about to be fired and he had to make some kind of a mark. So he hit upon the idea that he would make a major acquisition. That is not too hard. What you do is call up various investment bankers and tell them you are looking for a large acquisition. They make money by getting their percentage commission on the deal. If it is a small multi-million-dollar company, they make a smaller percentage, but it is still a lot of money. They could care less whether the deal works or not. They just want to close it.

If they get a guy like Price who is desperate to close a deal, and the investment bankers want to close the deal, then the board has a very serious problem. Your board of directors may not get the right information, or an independent evaluation of the pros and cons of the proposed acquisition.

Hughes: Why would this be something that a person like Price, in a precarious position, would want to do?

Gumbiner: Perhaps you are like a lot of people who do not understand this part of business.

Hughes: I want you to state your answer here, because there will be people reading this book who don't come from a business background.

Gumbiner: The big deal these days is acquisition or merger. Some people think bigger is better; don't worry that less than one half of acquisitions work out. Price wanted to be a big deal. He wanted to make a major acquisition or merger so that he would look like a wonderful, progressive chief executive. So he got together with the investment bankers and they found TakeCare.

Now, Jack Anderson had been trying to peddle this company to a lot of different organizations. I found out later that he tried to peddle it to Blue Cross and some other folks, because he had dressed it up for sale. He was not charging enough for his programs and he was paying the doctors too much--two major problems. He had no management and the company was not growing; nothing was happening.

Hughes: What is behind that statement, "dressed up for sale"? How do you camouflage these things?

Gumbiner: Easy. You don't put any money into future development and acquisition--no research, no development, no backup management, no training. Instead, you drop that money to the bottom line. Then you turn around and increase the volume by a number of [consumer] bodies by undercutting the market and not charging enough for your product. So since you have very little management in place, you are spending less. You cut your costs, but you can't go on very long that way, because there is no future. You dress it up for sale by increasing the net profit through removing departments and functions you need to develop and grow, and increase sales by under pricing. Then you figure you are going to sell the company within a year so you will not suffer the consequence. You cut off all your research and development, your marketing, all your management training, all these costs that you would have for a long-term organization.

You drop that money to the bottom line. It looks like you are making money, but you have a shell ready to crack.

I asked Anderson, "You don't have any backup for the chief executive. What would you do if you lost him?" He said, "We would have to scramble." I said, "That's not a good answer."

Negotiating the Deal
[Interview 2: February 13, 1996]

Gumbiner: In the fall of 1993, Hacken and Price flew down to see Anderson in Florida to convince him to sell TakeCare to FHP rather than to United Health Care. Eventually they came up with a proposed deal, but the board and I didn't like the price, so we canned the deal and TakeCare went back on the block again.

Then Price and the underwriters revised the offer to a higher price. The investment bankers have a way of going back and manipulating the figures to show you that you can pay more for the company and in the end, in some way, it will work out. In retrospect, here is where we should have gotten an independent advisor to evaluate the soundness of the program.

In about December, 1993, I told Price and Hacken I was scheduled to go on a vacation over Christmas. I didn't conceive that anything would happen over Christmas on a deal that they had been working on for only a month. "No," they said, "nothing is going to happen for sixty days on this." I moved this vacation from Christmas week to New Year's week to make sure. "No, nothing is going to happen for sixty days," I was again reassured. So I left and went on a cruise on the west coast of Malaysia.

I no sooner got on the ship than I started getting faxes from these guys telling me that they were trying to close this deal with a letter of intent. I don't know whether Hacken was in on the deal or if he was just not very bright. I believe that Price, along with Hacken, tried to close behind my back so I couldn't question the validity of the assumptions.

The sum and substance of this is that they wanted to close the offer immediately. I told them, "You guys told me nothing was going to happen for sixty days. I'm not going to come running back to California on the chance that something is going to happen in the next two weeks." So the whole board flew out to Singapore with a legal advisor (on the company's dollar) to discuss this preliminary offer with me.

I really didn't have the data and was unable to focus on the deal, but I was confident that the rest of the board members and management had done their work. I felt that a preliminary offer was not a problem since, based on further investigations, we could actually drop the deal.

That was also a mistake. I don't think that good due diligence was done. I understand from some people just lately that the due diligence team had the information that TakeCare was undercharging the consumer and overpaying the doctors, but it never got past Price and Massimino. That information was stopped from ever getting to the board or to myself.

Hughes: Because they wanted the acquisition, regardless?

Gumbiner: Yes. We didn't get good information.

I think that another mistake was made right there by myself. That is, I should have hired a group of people to investigate Jack Anderson and his history in management and acquisitions. I remember at a board meeting when we were considering this deal, there was a question of Jack Anderson [TakeCare] getting two seats on the board. At least one or two the board members questioned that. I said, in my naivete, "Well, we have a nine-member board. So what if they have two seats out of nine? We have seven."

Now, on the surface, this would appear to be a reasonable assumption. However, subsequently one of our board members [Richard Rodnick] resigned, so we didn't have seven; we had six. So all they had to do was get two of our members to swing over to their side and they had four. Now we didn't have nine board members; we had eight. They had four [supporters] and I had four.

It ended up finally as four and four. I had myself, Burke Gumbiner, Bill Price, and Mark Hacken on one side. They had Jack Anderson, his nominee Richard Burdge. Then they swung over Joe Prevratil and Warner Heineman, particularly Joe Prevratil, who was able to influence Heineman.

Hughes: Why was that?

Gumbiner: I have no idea. Heineman was fundamentally a chief loan officer at Union Bank, and he really wasn't much of a manager. Allegedly, he was in on the original coup to get rid of Price and me two years after I resigned as CEO. Prevratil alleged that he had turned him around and therefore broken the coup. Why I didn't pay more attention to that, I have no idea.

Just before we closed the TakeCare deal, I managed to get the board of directors to vote a by-laws change increasing the board size from nine to eleven members and began a search for two more qualified board members. Another mistake was made here, in that we should have elected two knowledgeable members at that meeting, probably doctors.

I would advise anybody, if they are going to put an unknown person on their board, they should have a dossier on that person: the date they were born, everything that they did financially, businesswise and so forth. It appeared later that Anderson had made similar deals where he had sold a company and then taken over another acquired company. I hadn't really figured that out. If you find out something like that, then you don't let that person on your board.

Incidentally, I had inquired about Anderson in our Washington [legislative] office and amongst people in the industry, but without a formal inquiry, learned very little.

Hughes: You also were apparently critical of the attorneys who were advising you. I have a quote from a letter that you wrote in September, 1995: "The large amount of money we spent on attorneys advising us on how to defend a traditional take-over had nothing to do with what happened."13 Meaning that it turned out to be a back-door takeover?

Gumbiner: That was [the gist of] the letter that I wrote to Mike Weinstock, who was our corporate attorney. He had spent eons of time and thousands of dollars setting up takeover defenses to keep predators from buying our stock and taking a dominant board position. The letter was not critical of the attorneys who were in on the TakeCare deal; it was just critical of our corporate attorney. He had not paid any attention to the possibility of a back-door deal. All he had to do was pick up the telephone and say, "Dr. Gumbiner, as chairman of the board, I think you should pay some attention to the problem that you may be subject to a back-door takeover and that Anderson is attempting to influence your board members."

Hughes: What do you have to say about the price that was paid? There were two offers made. The first time around, it was sixty-two dollars and fifty cents per share, and then within a matter of months the offer was raised to eighty dollars.

Gumbiner: I think sixty-two-fifty was probably too high, to tell you the truth, to pay for TakeCare. I think we should have let it go to somebody else. The problem was that Anderson was a good negotiator and was negotiating with Price, who was not a good negotiator. I was not in on it. Now, whether it was Price trying to keep me out of it, or my own natural desire not to get involved, or simply timing, since I thought that I had plenty of time to step in before it closed, I don't know. I probably should have been negotiating with Anderson as one chairman to the other chairman, not leaving it up to the CEO. Besides, comparable share price is not the only pricing factor; we should have evaluated a number of other criteria.

I think the board was being manipulated by the CEO and the investment bankers because he needed brownie points and they, as I said, wanted to get the deal done to pick up their commission.

Hughes: What was the logic for substantially increasing the offer per share?

Gumbiner: The logic was that we were in a bidding war with United Health Care and they theoretically were offering more on an all-stock deal. It's like, "Going, going, gone." If you don't offer more, the other people will get the prize. Anderson got such a sweetheart deal, I couldn't believe it. He got preferred stock; he got common stock; he got a couple of board seats. We should have just told him, "This is all we are going to offer for this company, and if you don't like it, sell your company to somebody else."

At the time, I don't know what the confusion was, but I was personally pretty confused about what was going on, and I believed the investment bankers. I don't believe I fully understood the offers, nor did all of our board members. We had a couple of board members that wanted to do the acquisition. Price wanted to do the acquisition. They were willing to pay almost anything. Some investment bankers say we gave up a year's earnings to do this, which was a mistake.

In retrospect, we probably should have acquired a smaller, 20,000- to 50,000-person HMO, and let these big deals alone.

I should have realized that Price and company were not up to managing that big of a company.

Hughes: There is another quote here from you, again to do with money. You said: "Health care reform, particularly pushing Medicare into managed care units, will put a lot more money--and you stressed that--"on the table and thus, in the broader context, takeovers of this type will be a greater concern."14

Is there a lesson there as well? Because certainly there is a lot of money at stake here.

Gumbiner: It is simple mathematics. If you get $400 per person per month and you enroll 10,000 in Medicare, that's $4 million a month. That's a lot of money for not that many enrollees because of the high utilization cost, but the per sale cost is relatively low. Not only that, but you are being paid by the federal government, and that's like being paid with a government bond. Plus, you are being paid before you supply the service, i.e. the first of the month. When there are a lot of people trying to get that business and when there is a lot of money at the table, a lot of bad things happen.

Hughes: During the TakeCare merger, there were a lot of similar mergers going on in the health care industry.

Gumbiner: I wouldn't say a lot of similar mergers. There were other mergers and acquisitions going on but few that large. On the surface this one made perfect sense since the two organizations were complimentary; TakeCare was in Northern California and Colorado and FHP was not. I think that probably we really needed the advice of a good acquisition person that had been in big acquisitions as to what we were doing there and what the potential problems were.

Hughes: Do you think the other mergers were better advised?

Gumbiner: I don't know. Let's face it, when you get advice from an investment banking group that is only going to make millions of dollars if the merger goes through, you are not getting objective advice. They are interested in putting that deal together, no matter what. If it is not a good idea to put somebody on your board from the acquired company who could be a problem, that doesn't mean anything to them. If you are going to pay eighty dollars a share when you should be paying sixty dollars a share, they could care less. As a matter of fact, they would rather close the deal for eighty dollars a share, because they are being paid on a percentage of the deal and they will make more.

I would advise making a flat-rate deal with your investment banker, not a percentage deal. Percentage deals are not in one's best interest. The more money on the table, the more they attempt to close the deal, any deal. I think what you need is a second opinion from people who are not in on the deal and will give you an objective opinion. I thought I had that from at least one of my board members [Richard Rodnick], who had been in the merger and acquisition field. But, in retrospect, I think he had probably been in smaller acquisitions and also may have been affected by the emotional factors, i.e. the chase and the prestige. I just think we needed another dispassionate, objective opinion of whether this was a good deal or not for the company and how it would work out.

TakeCare Moves to Take Over

Hughes: The events which you view to have paved the way for TakeCare to take control of the board was the elimination of the Office of the President and termination and humiliation of Mark Hacken.15

Gumbiner: Yes. That was a power play by Anderson, just to see how far he could go in controlling my board members. If he could arrange that, then he knew he was lined up to maybe take over.

Hughes: So that was a psychological move?

Gumbiner: It was just a power play. The existence of the Office of the President didn't make any difference. Hacken's agreement was over in November [1995] and he was removed in June. He only had--July, August, September, October--about four months to go. So it didn't make any difference in the long run whether they eliminated him in June or they just didn't renew his contract in November. The only difference it made was a test of Anderson's strength, of whether or not he could turn two of my board members. Of course, he could get Price to vote for the elimination of Hacken, and once he did that, he knew that he had a good chance of taking over the company. Your comment on the termination of Hacken is an astute one because I believe that was part of the Anderson long-range plan to get rid of Hacken and thus decrease the FHP loyalists.

Corporate Culture Clash

Gumbiner: Several things happened before that were significant. When we acquired TakeCare, we knew that we had a totally dissimilar cultures, and we expected to assimilate them into the FHP culture. They were only interested in short-term gains. They were not interested in innovation, growth, developing management, and they weren't that interested in quality of care or marketing. They had grown by acquisition, not building, and knew nothing about health care, being IPA brokers (i.e. insurance people), not staff model providers.

In my view, we were unable to change their culture because they still had the same leadership. The only way to have done it would have been to fire their senior managers, (all of whom had golden parachutes), and replace them with FHP managers. In the words of Machiavelli's book, The Prince, "Kill the ruling family."

It is very difficult to merge two companies unless the culture of the company that has been acquired is changed to correspond with the acquirer. Obviously, the acquirer is more successful than the acquiree, or they wouldn't be able to acquire. In order to do that, they have to eliminate the leadership of the company that has been acquired by removing its management and replacing those people with the management of the company that is doing the acquiring. Otherwise, it will be impossible to merge the two companies since it will be impossible to discontinue the attitudes, customs, and cultures of the acquired company and replace it with those of the acquirer.

I failed to do this, and what is even worse, in some instances, I moved their management in over ours; for instance, in Denver, in California, and in our EDP [electronic data processing] Department. I was thinking that we could utilize any good managers they had and retrain them, but this was a big mistake.

Most important, when you bring some TakeCare board members onto your board, you are bringing their culture and their thinking onto your board. This can fatally wreck the direction and focus of your board because it creates defection, particularly if you are bringing on very focused and aggressive people from their board. They will attempt to change your board to their culture. Therefore, the chairman must continually communicate with the board of directors and evaluate the board members, removing the disloyal, the incompetent, the hostile. It is important to make sure that you have your friendly votes and do not have any undermining from your board members, particularly from the board members you acquire from the other company.

The best thing is to never acquire those board members. If you are paying a premium for the other company, then their board members should not be allowed on your board. Some might say that you are developing a board that doesn't contribute and doesn't question your management or your chairman, but on the other hand, you wish to have constructive criticism, not destructive undermining and plotting by people who have an agenda to destroy your company's direction.

In balance, the chairman is better off to have friendly votes to get things done and preserve the culture. As the founder and chairman gets older and loses interest and has decreased energy, it is even more important to have a plan to retain power and a good succession program. Otherwise, the younger, more energetic management who are hungrier will line up the board members--there are always some envious or dissatisfied members, those who imagine slights or insults—and attempt to depose you, which is an age-old problem.

Be sure you can control the information. Information going to the board of directors should always go through the chairman to clear it for accuracy and make sure there is not some secret agenda. The chairman must remain in control if he wants to stay around. The chairman must plan for succession if he wants to go. Obviously, he must go some day. Therefore, it is important to have a succession plan so that the policies, the mission, the philosophy of that company continues.

Hughes: You said that before the acquisition TakeCare was actually three companies, three not very well integrated companies.

Gumbiner: Exactly. There were three acquired companies that were somewhat disorganized and disintegrating, not integrated. So I made another mistake there when I leaned too much on my management people for advice. You have to remember, I wasn't trying to run this company; I was trying to be the chairman. As I remember, I gave them some bad advice. I said about the TakeCare management, "Why don't we just try to use them? Because if they have any management talent, we can use it." Naively, I was thinking that they were on the same wavelength that I was, that they were going to try to work together with us and build a bigger and better company, when in fact that was not what they were up to. They were up to taking over our company. There is a total difference there.

[R. Judd] Jessup, the former CEO of TakeCare, then became a pipeline for Anderson getting all the information he needed about the company, whenever he needed it. Since Price was weak and timid, and Jessup didn't know much about the business but he was aggressive, it was easy for Anderson. I would advise anybody that when they acquire a company like that, they fire all their chief executives and put their own executives in their place. That is the only way to change their culture. We couldn't change their culture because their executives were there. Remember, we didn't have a strong central corporate entity and we didn't have the matrix system anymore--Price had destroyed that.

Hughes: When you acquire a company, one of the things that you acquire is management expertise. So what you are doing, in a sense, is cutting your profits by paying top dollar for supposed expertise that you then dismiss.

Gumbiner: You could take that position only if you are as naive as I was. The clue was that when Anderson negotiated the deal, he negotiated golden parachutes for his ten top managers. If he were I, he would have fired them. You cannot change a culture if their management is still in place. Their culture had been there too long. Their culture was to get short-term gain by liquidation instead of by building. If you have somebody like that who is not interested in going together with you in building a bigger and better company, and they are interested in doing it their way, I just think you are better off firing their top management and putting your top management in there. Besides, we didn't acquire them for their management but for their enrollment, their market.

If we had had our matrix system, it would have been a piece of cake, because our marketing people would have imposed our marketing policies on them. Our financial people would have imposed our financial policy on them. Our operating people would have imposed our operating systems. But we didn't have that.

Hughes: Are you sure that that is good advice across the board? I would think that yours is a radical position.

Gumbiner: I'm sure of it. If their management is still in place, they are going to keep going towards their goals and policies, not yours.

Hughes: You don't believe that there are cases where one of the rationales for the merger or acquisition is because the company being acquired recognizes that the philosophy and vision of the company acquiring them is more suited for the particular business context?

Gumbiner: Well, that's in all the textbooks, but it is wrong! That is one of the textbook reasons for acquiring a company. If you don't have enough management and they have management, you acquire them for their management. But in this case they only wanted to sell their stake to the highest bidder, i.e. to make money not to build a company.

You acquire management only if you want to give up your policies. We were a very strong, vibrant organization with good management depth. We knew which way we were going. We had a policy. TakeCare was weak in management with no depth. They had no orientation towards innovation and growth. I am just saying that if you want this idea of merging cultures of two companies to be successful, you get rid of all their senior management. Then you have a good chance of merging the cultures, because now you have put your senior managers in their managers' place, and now you can merge them and you can make the culture work. In any event, we didn't do that.

The Northern California Market

Gumbiner: The major reason I had agreed to this acquisition was because TakeCare had 300,000 commercial members in Northern California, and I wanted to enroll 300,000 Medicare members there. The existing 50-50 rule meant that I needed the 300,000 commercial members in order to enroll the 300,000 Medicare members. That was the major reason I agreed to this. I wasn't that concerned about the enrollment they had in Denver, Ohio or Illinois and planned to sell that immediately.

Hughes: So you saw the Northern California market as the plum?

Gumbiner: That's right. It was simple mathematics. If you enroll 100,000 new Medicare members in Northern California at $400 per member per month, you raise your return to your shareholders by twenty or thirty cents per share annually, a significant amount.

But that never happened. Price, for some reason, never put the right management people in Northern California. He put untrained FHP people up there, and TakeCare continued to run their Northern California operation just the way they always had, without coordinating with FHP, and FHP never took advantage of the major reason for the acquisition.

Hughes: Also, wasn't there a delay in getting approval to expand into Northern California?

Gumbiner: Yes, in some counties. But in some of the counties TakeCare had the right to enroll Medicare, but they just weren't doing it. If we had eliminated their management and put our strongest managers in, we could have done it. I would have put the strongest manager we had up there, with marching orders: "I want 50,000 Medicare members within six months or a year. I don't care how you get them. You can get them through the TakeCare system; you can get them through the FHP system, and if you can't get things done in Washington, pour on the heat, get it moving in Washington. Whatever you have to do." But Price didn't do that. He wasn't focused or dynamic enough.

Hughes: Plus the fact that he didn't have the Washington legislative office at that point.

Gumbiner: No, we had it at that point. The Washington legislative office didn't go until Anderson took over. This could all have been done in the time between closing the TakeCare deal in June of 1994 and Anderson's takeover, which was in June of 1995.

In the spring of 1994, we already had a small FHP operation up in Northern California where we were not doing too well because of weak local management. When we finalized the TakeCare deal, we had 300,000 TakeCare commercial enrollees in Northern California, which we could have used to bring in another 100,000 Medicare members. However, as I understood it, not all the counties that TakeCare and FHP were in had permission to enroll Medicare members. They were trying to get authority to merge FHP and TakeCare from the California Corporate Commissioner. At the same time, they were attempting to get permission from HCFA [Health Care Finance Administration] to enroll TakeCare and FHP Medicare members in all the different counties in Northern California where they had commercial enrollment.

However, as I understood it, there were certain counties in which TakeCare had permission to enroll Medicare, and all we had to do was take over the TakeCare operation, remove their managers, put our management in, and consolidate it. It didn't make any difference if they were officially consolidated to go ahead and enroll Medicare through TakeCare, and that never happened.

Hughes: Now, you have given me two different ratios. You spoke of a 50-50 commercial-to-Medicare ratio, and just now you spoke of a three-to-one.

Gumbiner: I never said three-to-one; it's always been 50-50.

Hughes: I understood you to say that there were 300,000 commercial contracts, which allowed you to enroll 100,000 Medicare members.

Gumbiner: No, I didn't say that. I said there were 300,000 commercial contracts. We could have enrolled 300,000 based on the 50-50 ratio; we didn't plan to enroll 300,000. We planned to enroll 100,000, which would have brought in the necessary gross revenue to justify the acquisition.

Hughes: So that wasn't a legal decision; that was a business decision.

Gumbiner: And the market wasn't up there for 300,000.

Hughes: Do you want to talk about your resignation?

Gumbiner: My resignation was the result of the Anderson TakeCare takeover. It was obvious that I wasn't going to be able to reverse things immediately without expending a lot of energy, and I was very ill with complications of my recent surgery--under treatment for infection. My doctors were telling me that if I continued to be stressed out and fight with these people, that I wouldn't get well. So I made the decision that the most important thing in my life at that time was my health. If I had stayed on that board, I could not resist showing up at meetings and arguing with them to try to get the destruction turned around. It was fruitless at that time for me to do this; besides, I believed they would soon see a shareholders' suit.

But many things happened prior to that behind the scene. I think that what went wrong would be good lessons for CEOs, chairmen, and boards in managed health care organization acquisitions. The major problem was allowing TakeCare management to stay in place, which I think was a mistake since this precluded merging the cultures.

The other thing was the lack of speed and focus in accomplishing the planned strategy in Northern California. If I were focusing and concentrating on the merger activity, I would have been all over management to enroll Medicare in Northern California and get rid of the units in Illinois and Ohio. I personally should have flown up to Northern California with our CEO, interviewed [our managers], made a decision on whether or not they should stay, and given marching orders up there.

If I had done that, then I would have been the CEO again.

I was not getting paid to be the CEO, nor did I want to spend the time and energy, so why should I do it? So I was still depending on Price, and hopefully Hacken, being a surrogate for myself, to take care of it. I assumed, wrongly, that management understood why we had paid so much for TakeCare and what the objective was.

Well, Hacken didn't take care of it. Hacken was as bad as Price in being timid and indecisive. Behind the scenes, Massimino was encouraging Price to roll over Hacken, to keep information from him, frustrate him and get him to quit, because Massimino had his own objective in controlling Price.

Meanwhile, Joe Prevratil, a board member, was playing a role. He had a meeting with my son Burke where he tried to use him as a messenger to me to not oppose the takeover, and suggested to Hacken that he quit. Somehow I couldn't believe it and didn't act. So somewhere in there this other underhanded stuff between Prevratil and Anderson was in progress. I don't know what was going on there, but Prevratil was working for Anderson out here on the West Coast.

Interestingly enough, somewhere in 1994, probably in the fall, somebody had a birthday party for Anderson in Texas to which they invited Price, Heineman, and Prevratil from my board, but they didn't invite me and they didn't invite Burke. That should have been another clue that something wrong was going on, but I still didn't act.

I have no idea how Anderson did this, to tell you the truth. He had to have a lot of cooperation from this fellow Prevratil, to work on Heineman here. I can't conceive that Anderson could do it by telephone from Connecticut. So he was working two ends. He had his ex-CEO Jessup, who was in charge of California, feeding him information, and had Prevratil working the board.

Toward the end, Price and Massimino independently had decided to move Jessup down a notch because he was failing as a manager, and to take him out of being in charge of California and put him someplace else. As soon as Anderson got wind of that after the takeover, Jessup was moved right back up to being in charge of California again. He immediately fired most of the FHP senior managers in California. The last I heard he was trying to manage twenty-four different direct-report managers. He fired all of the managers in Riverside; he left a young manager out there to run something like twelve or fifteen IPA networks. That person did not do anything because he could not manage that many reporting managers.

The name of the game is called "managed care." If you don't manage the IPAs, do the prior authorizations, and check on availability, you don't have a managed care organization anymore. So I don't know how they can survive. Besides, everyone knows that a company is measured by its management quality and depth.

Lessons Learned from the Back-door Takeover

Gumbiner: For the record, I would like to warn other people who are in the position that I was, after being the founder and CEO of a company for a number of years. If they want to become the chairman in the traditional manner and to step aside and allow someone else to be the CEO, they should be aware of potential problems. In my situation, the lack of knowledge of these dangers ended up in a takeover and dismember of the company. I think serious mistakes were made in three different areas.

Need to Assess a Proposed Acquisition

Gumbiner: The first mistake was made in the acquisition area. The TakeCare acquisition was simply too big an acquisition for our organization to digest, particularly with the management that we had on board. No one, including myself, paid enough attention to due diligence in relation to the type of people we were joining and what their motivations were. This could easily have been evaluated and forecasted by looking at TakeCare's history. If we had obtained a good history of what they had done, particularly of Mr. Anderson, we would have figured out that he was more of a predator than he was a builder of companies.

The acquisition teams that we sent to TakeCare were naïve or not knowledgeable enough, and somehow their findings were not conveyed to me or the board. I think it was filtered by the [FHP] management, who desperately wanted to make the acquisition, and the board never got good information. Perhaps the board depended upon management and management did not do the job. Definitely, a board committee should control the investigation process and due diligence.

Equally important would be a second and even third opinion from an investment banker who is not involved in receiving a commission. An independent consultant should also be involved as to whether the price you are paying in cash and in various types of stock, warranties, and so forth, is too high. I think that the acquisition was not carefully investigated enough. We did not have adequate independent consultation or teams of our people visiting to evaluate how TakeCare was managing and what their objective and culture was.

The second mistake was the way in which we attempted to merge the two companies. The mistake there was made in leaving the TakeCare senior managers in place, which meant it was almost impossible for us to change their culture. There should have been a better plan on how to merge the companies. We should have known that we needed to remove their senior management and identify our people to put in their place. I believe that instead of our better management going to Texas, which was a sinkhole, they should have gone to Northern California to replace the TakeCare management.

Lastly, I think the back-door takeover itself, in which the acquired company's chairman became the acquiring company's chairman and imposed his philosophies on that company, was identical to a frontal takeover, in which he would have bought enough stock to control the company and impose his own philosophies. That back-door takeover could have been avoided. We attempted to make sure it would not happen when we increased the number of board members from nine to eleven at the time of the acquisition. Unfortunately I did not fill the new positions at that time. In retrospect, we probably should have increased the seats to fifteen and filled them immediately. Stacking the board is a pretty familiar tactic, ever since FDR [Franklin D. Roosevelt] tried to stack the [U.S.] Supreme Court. He could not deal with them, so he enlarged it. It would have been very simple for us to fill those eleven seats; I should have filled them with people I could trust, and most importantly, who had our visionary philosophy.

[FHP] being a health care provider, we should have had more doctor representation from the staff model on our board of directors. That would have preserved our objectives as a health care provider, not as a vehicle of creating wealth for investors.

Hughes: You didn't have any doctor board members except for yourself?

Gumbiner: No, and that was a mistake. I believe that we probably should have enlarged the board to fifteen and elected only those people who were loyal and had the same objectives as we had in building a health care delivery company for the benefit of providers and consumers. Then we could have taken our time to look for qualified outside board members and deleted those board members who were not with us, did not understand business, or who had personal wealth creation as their main objective and not the long-term benefit of the company.

Hughes: Including the two TakeCare board members?

Gumbiner: For instance, part of Anderson's deal was that he and Burdge would be on the board and he would be renominated.

Now we could have simply nominated him after one year. His tactics would have made a reasonably good case not to renominate him. He could have sued us for damages, but we could have made a case that he was destructive and counter-productive as a board member. That could have dragged on for years, but he would have been out of there.

The Care and Feeding of a Board of Directors

Gumbiner: In my dealing with the board of directors, a mistake I made was that I did not reorganize the board. I did not like some of these people; I did not trust them; I did not feel that they were going the same direction that I was and did not know the business. If you do not have a board of directors that you can trust, respect, and feel confident with, I think you are making a mistake to keep them.

On the other hand, the care and feeding of the board of directors is a critical element. I had been chairman so long that I was not paying attention to the board of directors. I was concerned with my health and my personal affairs. Besides, I was bored and tired and I did not want to work that hard any more. I think that anyone that wants to stay chairman has to constantly schmooze the board members, even if he knows them well. That is all the more reason that he or she should like them and trust them. Because if the chairman does not like them and trust them, he is not going to want to spend any time with them. Therefore, one thing- feeds upon the other, and the board members become resentful, envious, jealous, and angry, so any lightning rod that comes up will cause a problem.

Hughes: What were your criteria for choosing board members prior to the acquisition?

Gumbiner: My problem was that I was attempting to locate qualified potential independent outside directors for key committees. The qualified board members that I was trying to find were people who had had experience in business, hopefully experience of being a chief executive officer of a large company in the service industry. Warner Heineman did not fit that at all!

The only thing that he ever did was become a senior vice president of the Union Bank, which did not qualify him to run any large company. He was put on the board at the request of another board member who later died.

On our board, we had one member [Gunther Klaus] who died, one resigned [Richard Rodnick] because of his problems on another board that took a lot of his time, and the third, Mark Hacken, resigned because he was finessed and bought out by the opposition. So things can happen to your board members.

I think you have to constantly look at your board members, and if you do not trust them or like them, and you do not think that they understand your business or understand the concept that the company is working toward, you should eliminate them as they come up for reelection, even if you have to put somebody in there that is not that prominent but who understands what is going on.

Need for Strong Management

Gumbiner: The second part of that was that I did not trust the [FHP] CEO. I thought he was devious; I thought he was incompetent, but I did not do anything about it. I suppose the chairman (particularly the founder), if he knows that people are not trustworthy and not competent, should recommend to the board that they be replaced, appoint a search committee, and get on with it.

Hughes: Were you faulted for not doing that?

Gumbiner: I fault myself for not doing that. Instead, I tried to prop up Bill Price by creating the Office of the President when I should have terminated him. The board was ready to terminate him and go on a search. For some reason, I did not do that. I think it was because I did not think it was easy to find a successor who knew the industry. I would be in the situation again of finding someone, orienting them, allowing time for success or failure, then perhaps having to repeat the process again if that person did not measure up. Besides, I thought the job was too big for one person.

Good advice would be to simply set guidelines. In other words, I would give a person a year, and if he does not achieve certain things in a year, then he is out of here. That is about the only way you can do it. So I would suggest that if you do not trust your management; you do not think they are competent, then you should get rid of them. Get people in there that you can trust and who can do the job.

Part of this is my fault because I was burned out, tired of the whole thing. I was not paying attention to it and I did not like some of the board members and management people, and they can usually tell pretty quickly when somebody does not like them.

Hughes: Maybe the lesson there is that even the chairman should have a definite term and meet certain criteria.

Gumbiner: That is probably right. As part of the whole procedure, you should have other people on the board who could become chairman and who understand the goals of the organization.

Justifying an Acquisition

Hughes: Why don't you talk about criteria for an acquisition? In your case, you thought the justification was the 50-50 deal with the commercial versus the Medicare membership in Northern California. The reason that you gave was that Mr. Price needed this acquisition for his own personal reputation. But there must have been other reasons for the takeover that perhaps can be generalized.

Gumbiner: I think that if you have a good company that is well financed and doing good things, the only reasons for an acquisition are: (1) you want to extend into another territory or another market, (2) you need their management, (3) you need their financing, or (4) you need the product or service and their enrollment. Companies would like to buy FHP because they would like to have the 300,000 Medicare members that FHP has.

Buying membership is also a way to grow more rapidly. Otherwise, if you were to enroll 100,000 people a year and you lose 30,000, netting out at 70,000, it would take you a long time to get to another 600,000 to 700,000 people. Whereas with an acquisition you would immediately get to that point by buying the bodies.

Some of these companies, like United Health Care Corp., do not really grow that much by marketing; they grow by acquisition. They trade stock for stock, but that is a self-generating thing. I can remember when United was a dog, but now they have grown by acquisition. The bigger they get, then the higher their stock price. The more successful they are, the more they can acquire another company less expensively, because they have stock that is of worth more in an exchange.

Hughes: What do you think of that method of company growth?

Gumbiner: I do not think much of it, because it creates a loose federation and does not build towards an integrated objective. I think some of it is just a result of popularity: everybody is doing it, so if you are not acquiring a company, then you must not be a very successful company. The theory is that the stronger companies swallow the weaker companies.

I think FHP should have acquired smaller companies. Pacificare acquires smaller companies--20,000 to 50,000—and that's the way to do it. They seem to have a good acquisition specialist on board who gets out there, tracking down these smaller companies, not just waiting for some investment banker to come up with something.

III. ROBERT GUMBINER'S RESIGNATION AND AFTER-MATH

The June 21, 1995 Memo16

Hughes: This morning we were talking about the events that led to your resignation. We talked about the seventeen-page memo which you wrote on June 21, 1995, and which presumably was sent to the members of the board. Who else received it?

Gumbiner: Maybe senior management. I don't recall exactly.

Hughes: What sort of reaction did you get?

Gumbiner: I did not get any. It is just like I dropped it in the well; like those two letters that I sent to the investors in December.17 They did not cause a ripple either. I expected at least to get a letter or two back, because there are dozens of investors.

One of two things could have happened. My letters could have gotten lost in the Christmas mail, but the one on the 28th should have found its way into the first-of-the-year mailbox. I think probably most people just scratched their heads and said, "Well, that's interesting; we'll see what happens," and put it in their files. As for the board of directors, I believe that the deal was set before my letter, promises were made, and they did not want to be bothered by reason.

Hughes: What could shareholders have done?

Gumbiner: Someone might have called me or sent me a fax and said, "Tell me more," or "What do you think of this and that?" Or merely said, "I disagree with you," or "You're all wet." But I got no reaction. It's almost as if it was never sent.

Hughes: Even worse from your standpoint was not getting a reaction from your own board members?

Gumbiner: I did not get one reaction from that seventeen-page letter. I got reactions from management staff saying, "I heard there was a letter out; I would like to read it." I think the die was cast by that time. I think Prevratil and Heineman were the only ones that Anderson needed and had already made up their minds to vote Anderson in and vote me out.

You have to realize that a good part of the reason was based on emotion. Heineman, for instance, always wanted to be head of the audit committee, but I never made him head. It was probably a mistake on my part, but I did not think much of him. I did not think he knew anything about management. I thought he gave the company bad advice, and I thought he was spineless. He made the motion to substitute Anderson for me, and when the meeting was over he said to me, like a child, "Well you thought I could never do anything." I said, "Well, you got that right."

So Heineman became head of the audit committee, for which he received $25,000 a year in addition to the $40,000 a year board fee. No one was ever paid anything like that before. I believe he also received a 25,000 share stock option.

Prevratil became head of the executive committee, for which he received $50,000 a year, in addition to the $40,000 a year board fee, with an option for 50,000 shares of stock.

So I think that Anderson had already made his deal and promises of paying these people off.

Hughes: You think that was Anderson's decision?

Gumbiner: Oh, yes. Anderson was the instigator and always works through other people. At the annual meeting on November 15, 1995, he did not sit on the dais with Bill Price. You would think a new chairman would be up on the stage telling everyone what his vision is for the company. No, he sat in the audience. He never made a sound. At the meeting where they got rid of Hacken, they had this fellow Burdge make the motion. When they got rid of me, Anderson had Heineman make the motion.

Hughes: Is that passing the buck?

Gumbiner: No, it is just the way he operates. He is not passing the buck. He is more like the monkey with the cat's paw, if you remember that story.

Hughes: No.

Gumbiner: The hot chestnuts are on the stove, and the monkey takes the cat's paw and takes the hot chestnuts off the hot stove with the cat's paw, not his own hand. That's just the sneaky way Anderson operates behind the scenes.

November 15, 1995 Annual Meeting

Gumbiner: Interestingly enough, the night before that meeting, Joe Prevratil came to my house to talk to me. I was pretty sick; I didn't think I could get through that meeting the next day because I had complications after my surgery and I was on antibiotics and really felt bad. He came over and said, "Bob, I want to tell you I'm your friend. I want to tell you they will get rid of you tomorrow. I suggest you resign tonight." Here is a guy that wants to absolve his guilt and get me to resign.

I said, "You know, Joe, I wish you would stop saying that, because you are not my friend. I want to tell you, when you were down and out, I gave you an office to work in. When they wanted to kick you off the board because you owed us $300,000 in health plan dues, I protected you. I gave you $2 million to get the Queen Mary[18] started, which you have been living on for the last two years. You are such an ingrate that you are going to come here and tell me that they, which is really you, are going to vote against me." I told him to leave my house. He left grumbling. I was just too sick and disgusted to deal with him and his type of mentality.

Hughes: Now, was that the first word that you had had about what might happen the next day?

Gumbiner: I think it was. See, the interesting thing was that I had not been able to make the Utah board of directors meeting, which was two or three weeks before that, and I was trying to get well. So I went to Palm Springs for four or five days, just to sit around and try to recover.

While I was gone, which was up to the day before the meeting, who knows what was going on? Prevratil, unknown to me, may have already made a deal with Hacken to resign from the board half an hour before the meeting, for $400,000 to $500,000 in stock options plus giving him some more stock options, as settlement for alleged wrongful dismissal from the Office of the President.

Hughes: That wrongful dismissal suit was pending?

Gumbiner: No, it was not pending at all. It was just something that they cooked up that Hacken might file. He never filed. It was just an excuse to give Hacken some money to get him out and get rid of his vote.

The funny thing was that I talked to Hacken two or three days before. I called him up and said, "Mark, I really need your vote. I want you to show up for this meeting." At the last board meeting, he had gone to the meeting in Utah but he had not gone to the dinner with these other directors that he was so mad at before the meeting. He also said, "Glad you canceled the board of directors meeting, because I can't stand those people."

I do not know what went on at the Utah meeting, but I think Prevratil and Anderson conspired over there and really worked on the takeover. Why Prevratil was dealing with Hacken rather than me as chairman is interesting. My illness, I think, played into their hands. You might say, "Why did they do it then rather than wait since it allowed you time to mount a proxy fight?" I think it was because they figured I could not fight back very well at the time.

Hughes: What was your son Burke's role in all of this?

Gumbiner: Burke didn't know anything about it, as far as I can see.

Hughes: Was he at the Utah meeting?

Gumbiner: Yes.

Joe Prevratil and the RMS Foundation/Queen Mary

Gumbiner: There was another thing that was playing into it. I had a falling-out with Prevratil regarding the Queen Mary. I had set up this project on lease from the City of Long Beach as a not-for-profit foundation, the RMS Foundation, and contributed $2 million to fund it. Prevratil was supposed to run the ship, because he had run it before for Wrather Corporation, and I was supposed to be the chairman and set policy. As a non-profit I could not realize any return on the investment, it was just something I wanted to do for the City of Long Beach and have fun with it.

Well, about six months into I realized that Prevratil did not know how to run the ship efficiently, and he had no vision or innovative ability. Besides, he was contracting for services and not putting them on the books. I found out that he had contracted for $1 million in advertising and had not paid these people, nor had he listed that as an account payable. I also found out that he was telling me that the restaurants were making money when they were losing money, because he was not putting any of the ship's overhead into their costs. I realized that no one would sue Joe Prevratil for "cooking the books" because he had nothing, but they might sue me, so I resigned from the Queen Mary as chairman of the board of directors within six months of taking it over.

Actually, I loaned $2 million to the Queen Mary, the RMS Foundation, which I set up to operate the Queen Mary, because in the beginning I could not give them the money since they were not yet a qualified not-for-profit. I had to wait until they got qualified. When they became qualified in the fall of 1994, I converted half of the money, $1 million, into a contribution. I placed a condition on that gift that they would have to give me accurate financial statements and a plan for what Joe planned to do to turn that thing around, and how close he was to the plan, i.e. what he was going to do with my grant. Putting a condition on a grant is a common practice to make sure the purpose is being accomplished.

Well, Prevratil refused to do that. He never gave me the financial information. He never gave it to the city. He was a year late with his financials [reports] to the city. As a result, I never contributed the other $1 million, so I was having a little bit of a to-do with him about that. I never anticipated I would ever get the money back, as he was about $5.5 million in debt on the project, living hand to mouth. I just wanted to know where my funds were going.

Prevratil may have been trying to get even with me, probably for severing my relations with the Queen Mary. Publicly I said I had other things I had to do, but privately I let him know I was leaving because I could not tolerate the way he was mismanaging the ship. I had expected to go in there and have a little fun building it up--put in water transportation, new decorating, new concepts for the restaurants, a cabaret in the art deco bar, unique shops, and an art center. He did not want to do any of that, or anything new, even though I commissioned two decorators and we decorated two or three suites to show what could be done. We redecorated his office, essentially on my money, which I never got back. So there was a certain amount of ill feelings between us, you might say.

Finally, after Prevratil helped engineer the back-door takeover, I met with him and said, "You know, Joe, I do not want to be on any board of directors with you. I do not want to have anything to do with you, and I would suggest that you get off the FHP Foundation board." By that time, which I did not know, he was chairman of the FHP Executive Committee, and instead of his leaving the board, he got the FHP Executive Committee to remove me from the foundation board. After founding and spearheading the foundation for ten years, I thought I was a fixture. The rest of the board was aghast--you saw the letter from the attorney for that board of directors.

FHP Restructuring Begins

Gumbiner: It is amazing. I went to the FHP Foundation board meeting [July 10, 19951, again I was not feeling well, and Warner Heineman was sitting there. I really did not feel that they could remove me. In other words, I think I should have served out my term, but I really was too sick to argue with them. Prevratil had dropped that bomb on them before I walked in, that FHP was replacing me with Warner Heineman. I decided to resign rather than argue. And the funniest thing happened: they all gave me a tribute, including Price. Price got up and made a speech about what a wonderful guy I was and how much I had done for the foundation. It was amazing.

Burke just told me the other day that they brought in two new board members, and Price did a board orientation for them in which he spent most of the time extolling my achievements. Was Price dealing with reality or not?

Hughes: Well, from his standpoint, doesn't it make good sense? Here's an institution that is building on a long history.

Gumbiner: Yes, but then they removed their chairman and substituted a whole different set of values. You would think they would say, "Well, we reversed it. Our chairman was okay for the time he was around, but he wasn't up to the times, so we have changed."

Hughes: But they didn't say that?

Gumbiner: No. They just said, "He was a great visionary..." But they do not say that they are not following that vision any more. It's really all very odd.

More on Care and Feeding of a Board of Directors

Hughes: What else should be said before we get to your resignation?

Gumbiner: I do not know what can be said about it, other than the fact that, if the chairman does not pay attention to the board and does not have good allies, he is in trouble. I thought I had an ally in Joe Prevratil, who eventually destroyed my policies and would not support me.

Previously, I had a fellow named Gunther Klaus who was on my board for years. He was a great supporter, and I could depend on him to defend my backside. While I was out leading the troops, I at least had somebody back home guarding the door; but unfortunately he passed away.

It turned out that Prevratil was part of the takeover, so I guess the lesson to be learned is that you should not take anyone for granted, assume that they understand you, or that they have character. You have to stay close to everybody. It is hard work if you are chairman. You have to work at it. You cannot just sit back. I do not know how people like Ted Turner do it. They must work with their board constantly and put in a lot of time and energy to make sure it is dominated by loyalists.

Hughes: I certainly take your point of why a chairman needs board members that reflect his philosophy, but isn't there also a danger in having a board of yes-men or yes-women? I would think that one of the reasons that a chairman has a board is to get advice from a variety of viewpoints.

Gumbiner: Well, that's right. But once you decide to go one way, then the board should be together on it. There should not be divisions and people trying to undermine policy. Frank and open discussion and constructive criticism is good, but cloak-and dagger secret politics and manipulative behavior is bad.

The other mistake with many boards is they do not have people that understand its business. We did not have people that really understood the medical or HMO business. That was a mistake. Maybe you should have more board people that understand your industry. I also think the board probably should have term limits, if not written down, at least understood. I think a couple of terms is enough and they should be out of there. Otherwise, cliques form for counterproductive purposes. It should be a policy to regularly refresh the board by putting new people in there with new and different ideas. Most importantly, make sure that you do not have board members that have different agendas that are not in the best interest of the organization.

I wrote an article that was printed in the <u>Director's Monthly</u>[19] about why I felt that the policy of board members of public companies owning stock was a bad idea. It seems to be the current, popular idea that board members should own stock or have stock options, and therefore the board members will be interested in the stock price appreciation and the welfare of the investor.

Well, that is just the wrong angle from my view. I think board members should not own stock, because that makes them short-sighted. It's strange, but let's say they have options on 10,000 shares of stock. This will cause them to make decisions more for short-term stock gains than they will toward long-term development of the company. So I think they should not own stock in any form. They should simply be paid a reasonable professional fee, and they should be interested in serving on the board. No director should be paid an amount per year equal to more than 10 percent of his annual income, otherwise, he/she becomes dependent on that directorship income and can be manipulated to vote by implied threats to remove them.

That is a little contrary to what the general thinking is right now, but it begs the basic question, and that is, who does the company serve? Is it the greedy shareholder, or is it the customers and the loyal staff who are the major stakeholders? Shareholders should get a reasonable return on their investment but not at the expense of destroying the organization or affecting the quality of service.

Board Composition

Gumbiner: There is a lot of general thought about organizing boards and who should be on a board. There are boards that have a large number of people, and they try to include a certain number of women, a certain number of ethnic minorities, and so forth. I often wonder, how can these boards possibly work? These people are not selected for their ability to contribute to the company's policy; they are selected because they represent certain segments of the population. I would imagine in those boards, most policy is predetermined behind the scenes.

Then there is also a controversy that goes back and forth about whether the chairman of the board and the CEO should be one and the same person. On most European boards, the chairman is different than the CEO. On American boards, they tend to be the same person. If they are the same person, logically it is hard to get rid of an incompetent CEO if he is also the chairman. On the other hand, if you have one person who is the chairman and another person who is the CEO, you can have policy conflict between the two.

Now, if you have a good, strong chairman, which I now advocate, he controls the board and gets rid of the CEO if there is a problem or lack of competence. Because if he or she does not control the board, then there will be destructive friction and, if the CEO is incompetent, the chairman cannot get rid of him. On the other hand, all the CEO has to do is butter up a few members of the board and his job is secure, whether he is competent or not, if the chairman is not strong and decisive. So that is another problem.

Board Size

Gumbiner: Then there is the problem of the large board versus the small board. I used to be an advocate of the small board, seven to nine members. I am not an advocate of that any more, because it can too easily be taken over and manipulated by a few determined individuals for their self-interests. Now I think a board of fifteen is probably a little more appropriate. It is harder to create self-interest objectives with fifteen members. In this situation that we just went though, all Anderson had to do was to get two votes; he had two already, so he had to get two of mine. That was made easy by the small eight-member board.

Hughes: Why did you formerly advocate a smaller board?

Gumbiner: I favored the small board before because it is easier to deal with and you can get things done. Just the exercise of trying to set a special board meeting for fifteen busy people can get difficult. It would be a lot easier to set a board meeting for seven or nine people. To call up seven or nine people and explain your position is a lot easier than trying to call up fifteen.

Hughes: It's also easier for a chairman to control a small board.

Gumbiner: Yes, you would think so. On the other hand, it is easier for another determined person to stampede a small board. It would be more difficult for a takeover to occur with a bigger board because of more differences of opinion. So there are pros and cons on both sides of this question. You see giant boards for some companies of, say twenty-six people. You often see them on not-for-profit organizations. It is very unwieldy. You have a lot of people there that are mildly interested, or there for prestige or wealth, who are noncontributing. This board of directors' thing is a field in which there are published articles, associations, meetings, and so forth. But when you have a $4 billion company hanging in the balance, plus patients' welfare or staff's welfare, it is not an unimportant matter.

Protective Board Mechanisms

Hughes: Are there board formats that should be specific to certain industries?

Gumbiner: I do not know. That is a good question, totally unexplored as far as I know. So far, the format seems confined to corporate protection. We organized the FHP board in Delaware because you can't have a staggered board in California; your board has to be elected all at once, which provides a greater chance for a takeover. In Delaware, you can stagger your board so that a third gets elected every year, with a three-year term.

There is a difference between states on cumulated voting and non-cumulated voting. It is rather technical, but what it really boils down to is, you can vote all of your shares for all of the seats on the board. In other words, if you have 40 percent of the shares, you could vote 40 percent for A, 40 percent for B, 40 percent for C. In the other instance, you vote for 40 percent across the board. These strategies are to prevent takeovers where somebody can try to get control of the board and subsequently the company by acquiring a majority of the shares and electing a majority of the board members. What Anderson did was much cheaper for him, because he did not have to buy controlling shares.

Other protective mechanisms have been created. For instance, if someone acquires five percent of the shares of a public company, they have to file a special form that alerts the company and everybody else that you may be in a position to attempt a takeover. Conversely, there is no filing or warning for a back-door takeover. Anderson did not file anything saying that he was attempting to get control of the FHP board and the company.

It is one thing to retire as CEO and become chairman, but then how do you get out of being chairman? You're not going to sit there and be chairman until you're ninety-five years old or die at your desk. You should have a definite plan for eventually getting out altogether. If you don't make a definite plan, you are going to end up like I did--losing the company.

There should be a plan to replace chairmen, i.e., bring in a replacement who is given a certain [trial] time period and goals.

If he does not measure up, then he is out and somebody else is brought in with a scheduled evaluation and time period. The board should be in agreement with this, and the chairman should expect to have to step back in for a few months while the company is doing a CEO search, or their senior staff should be strong enough to run the company while they are doing the search.

Resignation Statement

Hughes: On June 22, 1995, the day after you wrote that long memo, you resigned, and you issued what you said in a later document was a carefully prepared statement based on consultation with lawyers.20

Gumbiner: There was a [press] statement, which I am sure you saw.21

Hughes: Yes. Do you remember your thinking in the way you worded your press statement?

Gumbiner: The thinking was pretty obvious. First, I sought legal counsel to find out what I could do about this [forced resignation], and they told me I could not do much about it. Frankly, I had a series of bad legal advisors. They could have told me I could have mounted a proxy fight before the annual meeting, which I later found out.

I said to the attorneys, "You know, I think that the board is going to disrupt this company so badly that the board of directors is probably going to get sued. I do not want to be on that board, first of all because of my questionable health, secondly, I do not want be involved in all of the stress, time, and energy in fighting this board, and third, I do not want the legal and moral responsibility." I did not agree with the amoral firing of loyal people and the destruction of the management team we had built for [corporate] growth.

So the reason we carefully prepared that statement was so that I could say what I wanted to say without any legal repercussions.

Hughes: And there weren't any?

Gumbiner: That is correct.

Hughes: How do you explain that? The stockholders could have protested.

Gumbiner: What would they protest about? They wanted their stock to go up.

There was an interesting article written by a Salomon Brothers' analyst [Robert Hoehn], who said getting rid of the staff model and selling the hospitals was a bold move, but will it work?[22] And that is essentially what the shareholders were doing; they were waiting to see if it would work. Most shareholders or fund managers do not understand the [HMO] business, so they do not know that when you remove the hospitals, the staff model will not work well. When you remove the staff model, the IPA will not work as well. Management of a successful HMO is very far from their knowledge base.

The Question of a Proxy Fight

Hughes: You and Burke [Gumbiner], in August of 1995, met with three attorneys to talk over whether you should engage in a proxy fight.

Gumbiner: At that time, I was still suffering from complications of surgery and infection. These attorneys told us that we would have to do an East Coast road show which would be time-consuming and stressful, so I made the decision not to do that. Of course, that was bad advice, because we could have sent in a slate any time prior to sixty days before the annual meeting and not sooner than 100 days.

They should have advised us to submit a slate of who we felt were trustworthy people. We could have subsequently decided whether to pursue the proxy battle. Instead of doing the road show, we could have sent television tapes on our position to people and had conference calls. We could have created a grassroots program from the consumers and employees who felt strongly about it to send to institutional investors.

My other advice to the reader is to not just take one attorney's opinion on things like this. Get multiple opinions, just like doctors encourage you to get second opinions before going in for major surgery. Yet people like myself go to one attorney or one law firm and take their advice as gospel. Based upon that brief half-hour or hour visit, we made a decision which was probably a bad decision.

Probably if I had waged a proxy fight, I would have at least shown people that I cared about the company and I was trying to get control back. Even if I lost, it would have been better.

Plus it might have frightened a couple of the board members that were waffling, the Prevratils and the Heinemans of the world.

When [Carl] Karcher--I talked to his lawyer--went back to Carl's Jr. and threatened a proxy fight, a couple of the board members changed their votes because they did not want to get involved in that, and he was able to put a surrogate [chairman] in. In other words, he did not regain the chairmanship, but he had the financial guy that was bailing him out of his personal financial problems become the chairman but kept Carl Karcher's philosophy and policy. That's a middle ground. You can bring somebody else in as chairman, but on the provision that they are going to continue your philosophies.

Physician Management Company versus Staff Model Care

Hughes: In June, 1995, FHP began major restructuring, which we have talked about on and off through these discussions, but let's go through the points of restructuring sequentially, starting with the new physician management company, which originally was supposed to be called Compucare and then was later renamed the Talbert Medical Group.

Gumbiner: A physician management company has long been the dream of Jack Massimino, because he has always tried to figure out how he can personally get his hands on more money.

When we first capitalized FHP back in the early eighties, the board of directors wanted me to put up all of the money—I think it was perhaps $1 million. I did not want to do that because I felt that that would, first of all, not look very good, and second of all, I felt that everybody who had worked hard to put the company together during the twenty years it was not-for-profit should share in the future ownership.

So it ended up that I bought half of the shares, and the other half of the shares was offered to anybody who was a medical director or senior manager. There were about seventeen or eighteen of these people. At that time, they all bought into the company at a low cost per share. They were fully vested in two years after we converted. Later when the company went public, a certain number of them sold their stock and left. I thought that they would stick around to help build the company, but I was mistaken; many were shortsighted.

All of the managers who came in after that were what I call the "have-nots," and all of the seventeen or eighteen managers that were there were the "haves". The "haves" each had anywhere from $4 to $6 or $8 million worth of stock, and this caused jealousy from managers who came later but were the "have nots".

Jack Massimino had left us years ago for a better offer from a hospital consultant company, taking with him our HMO seat on the Certificate of Need board in Utah. He had been my assistant for a couple of years. Then I assigned him to manage Utah where he spent two years. He left us because someone offered him a little bit more money. So he is the kind of person that is always looking for more money. He ended up as a "have not" when he came back to the company.

Massimino was trying to figure out how he could get hold of some quick money. His plan, which I had heard of way before he thought of it, was to spin off the staff model into an old fashioned medical group, take it public, and then get his hands on a percentage of that stock and sell it, so that he could make several million dollars. That was his objective. So I was not surprised when he used Price and Anderson to help make that happen.

Anderson wanted to get rid of the staff model because it was management intensive, he did not know how to run it, and it was costly to acquire facilities. He did not know that it was the stabilizing influence that allowed the HMO to control the quality and availability [of health care]. The staff model/IPA combination allowed FHP to get ahead of the competition. He just wanted to sell it and then sell the membership to another HMO.

Hughes: What about the criticism of the staff model, that there are a lot of fixed costs and it's better to contract out?

Gumbiner: You cannot get quality; you cannot control access and cost when you are contracting out. You only can contract with the doctors you have in the community; you cannot get them to cooperate and you cannot get them to turn out quality work or to support the prepaid concept. Most importantly, you do not build a delivery system with just an IPA because there is not the capacity in the provider system to grow. Besides, someone has to "pay the piper". How can an outside medical group supply services any cheaper than your own medical group? They have to manage and pay personnel also. This does not make sense.

Hughes: And is that what you said to that criticism?

Gumbiner: Right. I said the IPA is totally unstable unless you have a staff model along with an IPA. We'll discuss it more, because it is important. My opposition kept trying to characterize me as wanting to hold on only to the staff-model provider mode when I actually had moved on to the combined staff/IPA model; the staff model to insure the IPA's success.

I had said, "You are not going to spin off the staff model." Price and Massimino could hardly wait to get Anderson in and get me out of there so they could take off and maybe grab that part of the company and stuff it in their pockets. That is exactly why it was done. It was not done because it was hard to run. If it was not worth anything, they would not want it. So what they are going to do is destroy FHP. Part of this began by firing the hospital-based doctors.

For instance, we had a system in our hospital where salaried nurse-midwives were on the OB [obstetrics] floors at all times. The nurse-midwives delivered all of the normal babies, but there was always a doctor, an OB/GYN [obstetrician-gynecologist] specialist, on duty on the floor twenty-four hours a day. Now they have fired all of the nurse-midwives and there is no doctor on the floor. So if a woman ready to deliver comes in, they have to find a doctor, just like the old-fashioned fee-for-service. I would have lost my granddaughter if that had been the situation, because they had to do a [Caesarian] section in ten minutes because the baby's heart rate went bad.

Hughes: That's a cost-cutting maneuver?

Gumbiner: Short-term, they get rid of the nurse-midwives' salaries, but it is more expensive in the long term, because now they have to have OBGYN doctors deliver all of the babies. Probably there was pressure from the doctors to protect their income.

I will give you another example. We used nurse anesthetists for all routine cases, supervised by an anesthesiologist. That way we got along with, say, three anesthesiologists and six nurse-anesthetists. They fired all of the nurse-anesthetists, so now they have to have six high-cost anesthesiologists. Does that make any sense? The nurse-anesthetists we had were on salary.

Other hospitals would not allow us to use nurse-anesthetists or nurse-midwives. So now you cannot have anything innovative because it is not allowed by outside-controlled hospitals. You cannot put your nurse-anesthetists or your nurse-midwives into somebody else's hospital. Then there were the hospitalists or doctors who only worked in the hospital covering intensive care and other patients 24 hours a day- superior accessibility and skills- all fired.

So let's go back to the question. Probably the most valuable asset of FHP was its staff model--the most difficult to construct, but the most valuable asset. And if run right, it could do the best financially and provide the best care. But since current management does not understand how to run it and they do not have the capability, what they are trying to do is to spin it off, take it public and then sell it and steal some of the stock. Or they would like to sell it to somebody else, put the money in their pocket, if management can get their hands on 10 or 20 percent of the stock for free.

Hughes: Sell the staff model, or sell FHP?

Gumbiner: Sell the staff-model company which has been separated from the parent FHP company.

Hughes: Have the physicians, nurses, and others who have chosen to stay been transferred into this independent medical group?

Gumbiner: They are literally working for that outfit.

Hughes: How do they feel about that?

Gumbiner: They do not like it very well, I can tell you that.

Hughes: Why?

Gumbiner: They do not like the leadership, because the management thinks that they are dealing with a commodity. They want them to see twice as many patients. They do not give them the necessary expensive equipment to work with.

Hughes: Does it indeed mean that the medical groups contract out to virtually any sort of health plan which happens to want them?

Gumbiner: They think that they can sell their services to other HMOs. I do not think that that is going to happen because I do not think other HMOs are going to contract with a competitor, i.e. if the medical group is owned 80 percent by FHP, a competitive HMO will not deal with them.

Hughes: So with whom does the medical group contract?

Gumbiner: They are still contracting with FHP.

Hughes: But that's not really the vision, is it?

Gumbiner: That is not their idea. Their idea is too phony up the books to make it look like they are making money and then sell the staff model. Remember, the people now running FHP are not builders; they are predators; they are sellers. They are selling off the carcass. They are going to sell a leg here, an arm there, a head over here, and so forth.

Hughes: You maintain that this is a reversion to a model which you believe was proved long ago not t o work?

Gumbiner: That's right. I have been there and done that. First, I tried developing a medical group, fee-for-service. That did not work. The doctors all fought over the spoils. Then I tried a group practice, prepayment that was a staff model. I tried a medical group that contracted with an HMO, and it was essentially a fee-for- service medical group. That did not work. That was destroyed in a big blow-up in 1966 and turned into a staff model HMO where everybody worked for the HM0.23 We were all working for the same goal. That worked well!

We then tried an IPA model in Guam along side the staff model that worked reasonably Well, since we controlled it with our staff model. We were practically forced into that. Then we started an IPA in San Pedro. FHP ended up in 1990 when I retired with about 60 or 70 percent of the FHP service in IPAs, backed up with the staff model. The IPA was easier for a salesman to sell because it was nothing new and different. The IPA just used the existing doctors, never mind that they may have been incompetent, were not available or were of the wrong specialty.

I will give you an example. In Utah they did not bill something like $3 million in services to Medicaid because they did not know how to bill. They just did not put it down in the billing. Our FHP people went over there and found it.

Hughes: What do you mean, they didn't know how to bill?

Gumbiner: They just did not know how to bill it.

Hughes: That doesn't make sense to me.

Gumbiner: Why doesn't it make sense to you?

Hughes: Well, how can a business group not bill for the services it provided?

Gumbiner: Because the service is provided by doctors and nurses and other providers who are not trained in billing and have no interest. A patient walks in the door who is covered by another insurance. But the wife is covered by FHP, so they just say, "Your wife is an FHP member?" They just charge it off to FHP when it is the other insurance that should have paid. The average fee-for-service hospital charges you for every little thing, right? They did not do that at FHP-Utah. They just say, "Here, take some medication, take a few catheters, take some blankets home." No charge is even written up.

That reminds me of when I was in Guam. Our manager needed some rubber heels for casts for our medical center. I was with her. So she went up to the government hospital and said, "I need some heels for casts." An employee said, "Here's a bag full." He did not charge her; he just gave them to her. She said, "Do you have any left?" "No." He gave her all of his heels for casts. He was not getting another shipment until the next boat came in. I was at FHP-Guam and the nurse said, "Here, you are cold; take the blanket home."

Mark Hacken set up a disposable medical equipment program because we were being stolen blind by contracting out. The outside medical equipment company was charging us for equipment, i.e. beds, etc., for people who had been dead for six months. When we canceled that company we found medical equipment we were paying for that didn't even exist.

As an example, I needed an IV pole when I was sick. They brought the IV pole out, but they never picked it up again. With poor management, FHP purchased $3 million worth of medical equipment--$1 million disappeared during the first six weeks. It was either stolen, given away, left someplace, or whatever. It was a good idea to provide and lease our own equipment, but it was not executed correctly.

A well-managed hospital will sometimes charge you for every Band-Aid, injection, et cetera. They do not do that at FHP. They do not know how to do that. They have never done it. They do not bill because they are set up for everything prepaid.

It is the same thing if you take care of every deadbeat that walks in the door. That is a big problem with fee-for-service, because people walk in, "That's going to be $150." "Oh, bill it to my insurance company, Doctor." "How do I know you have any insurance?" "Well, you can check on Monday." (This is Friday night or Saturday.) You check Monday; the guy does not work there [at the specified company]; he does not have insurance; he never had that insurance, or there is a $1000 deductible. He used to work there a year ago. Try to get paid after the service!

Hughes: There's also a culture clash: physicians, nurses, and other health professionals have presumably come to FHP because they either initially or as time goes on agree with the FHP prepaid philosophy.

Gumbiner: You put your finger exactly on it. Most of the physicians that came to FHP were recruited because they were tired of trying to run a business plus practice medicine. How are you going to tell them, "We want you to speed up and see more patients, and pay attention to every nickel and dime, be a bean counter"?

I hate to say it, but in a fee-for-service practice, you only treat people who can pay, because if you continue to treat people who cannot pay, you cannot pay your rent. Not only that, you throw in a few extra tests, because that is quality care, right? You are being very careful, so you run extra tests or do an extra procedure or have them come back two or three times for re-check, which you do not need to do.

The physicians practicing at FHP can take more time with the patient, but they do not have to have them come back two or three times to build up the bill or sell them the procedure that they do not need, et cetera. If you have a doctor that is avaricious and wants to make money, he would never join FHP, right? He would open up an office; he would sign up with every

HMO, and he would rush patients through, billing as much as possible.

I have seen fee-for-services practices. I saw one belonging to an ENT [ear, nose, and throat] man who was seeing a patient every five minutes. You talk about running people through: the fee-for-service doctors are the ones that run them through, because they have to, or they do not make any money. The doctors who are working for a salary, why should they rush anybody through? You cannot make them do it either, because they will say, "I can only see this many patients."

Hughes: Are there not quotas? Kaiser physicians, at least on the books, are expected to see a certain number of patients per hour, the number depending on their specialty. Was that not true at FHP?

Gumbiner: Well, we know that a general practitioner ought to see twenty-five or thirty patients a day. But as a general practitioner I know the business; I could have beat that easy. I could have all the little old ladies and men with hypertension who were not sick come in, and I would take their blood pressure, and have the kids that had an earache come back two or three times, and on and on. Have a nurse check blood pressure, and the patient is in and out of there in five minutes. That is the way I would see a lot of patients in a short time with no effort and refer the time-consuming patients to specialists.

The general answer to your question is that you must have overall production standards and guidelines. After all, it is poor care to allow a surgeon to take six hours for a procedure that should take one and a half hours. Something is wrong.

##

Gumbiner: Trying to do fee-for-service and prepayment at the same time is not successful because here is the patient that walks in and he is fee-for-service. Now you have to try to build the bill up and get as much money out of the visit as possible. Here is another patient that comes in who is prepaid, and you do not have to do that. So the doctor gets a little confused after a while.

Hughes: You have the same situation in the Talbert Medical Group. You are asking doctors to function in both roles, i.e., maximize the bill in one instance and not in the other.

Gumbiner: Exactly, because they think they are going to get fee-for-service patients off the street. They do not know how to bill and collect. They are not set up to check their insurance and manage coordinating insurance. The people that come in from the other health plans are not necessarily on capitation; we used to pay the IPA doctors on a fee-for-service basis, up to a maximum percentage of premiums, i.e. 26 percent. The more fees the doctors billed, the bigger their portion was of the percentage of premiums. So they were going to have to bill carefully for everything.

Some of the salary doctors do not want to do that. Within fifteen minutes they have to meet the patient, establish rapport, examine him, make a diagnosis, and prescribe a medication. That is a lot. And then you want them to try to keep track of all of the billing? Forget it. They will not do that. They will not put down a consultation. They will just put down a regular office call. That is what is going to happen.

And since their prepaid administration is not set up to make sure that everybody has insurance and to collect the 20 percent for the people who have a co-payment, they are not going to get that either. They are not going to collect the co-payment or the deductibles. It's going to be a disaster.

Elimination of FHP Hospitals

Hughes: Well another aspect of FHP restructuring was to get rid of the FHP hospitals. I know you have thoughts on that subject.

Gumbiner: All I can say is, you cannot deliver a complete health care program without integrating all of the aspects of care, the doctors, hospital, and pharmacy. Without a hospital, the managed-care system loses efficiency, control of quality, and the ability to initiate innovative cost-saving and quality systems. It is at the mercy of the outside hospital's profit motives and management.

Hughes: As part of your philosophy about vertical integration-

Gumbiner: That is not a new philosophy.

Hughes: I know it's not. But FHP leadership's new scheme is not new either.

Gumbiner: They are doing exactly the opposite of our long-term policy of vertical integration. They are "out-sourcing"--that's the new buzzword. When you out-source, you cannot keep control.

I will give you an example. My former wife [Josephine "Dodie"] had a stroke. The medics picked her up and took her over to St. Mary's Hospital. I called up FHP and said, "Look, I want a life-support ambulance out here and I want them to move her to the FHP facility." It is a better facility. You know how long it took a contract ambulance company to get a life support ambulance out? An hour and a half! So I said, "What the hell is wrong with you people?" The ambulance company said, "Well, we had to go find an intensive-care nurse, and we had to go to her house; she had to get dressed; we had to pick her up." I said, "By that time, you don't need an intensive-care nurse. The patient is dead!" So I said, "Forget it, FHP can't use your service."

That was our fourth or fifth ambulance service. They do not train their ambulance people right. After that, if we wanted a life-support ambulance, it came out of our hospital. A nurse from intensive care walked down the stairs and got aboard.

That was it!

Hughes: It is the conflict that keeps coming up: Between what you consider good medicine, and what your opponents consider economizing by contracting out.

Gumbiner: That is true, but what if you were the patient, the consumer, the customer, and your mother, wife, or husband had to wait an hour and a half for a life-support ambulance?

Hughes: Oh, I would be incensed.

Gumbiner: That's right. You would change health plans, wouldn't you?

Hughes: Yes.

125

Gumbiner: So there is a business reason for it. If you had to go into a hospital that is dirty, ugly, the food is terrible, and the service is poor, you do not care how sterile the surgery is.

I went down to Houston, Texas to have some cancer surgery done about a year ago. They were using a contract hospital. I would never go back there. I do not care how good the surgeon is. I selected the surgeon because he had the largest series of cases of that particular surgery in the country. You can imagine, I got a private room. It was noisy; they kept the door open and kept on the light. When I came out of anesthesia, they served me spaghetti and meat sauce for my dinner. Can you believe that? So you know what I did the next day?

Hughes: You checked out.

Gumbiner: I checked out, and I checked into a suite at the Ritz Carlton, and I ordered room service and had a nice bowl of chicken soup with a rose on the table. This suite cost me about $280 a night, and the hospital was costing me $1,100 a day. I was much happier.

But if you go to the average hospital, you will find that their food tastes terrible. I hired a chef at our hospital to direct the food service, and I was constantly unhappy. I used to watch the trays come back. If the trays came back full of food, I would have a word with the food service manager because the trays should not come back full of food. Either they are giving them the wrong foods, or it is poorly prepared, or there is too much of it. Why can't they give a post-op [postoperative] patient a bowl of chicken soup, right?

Hughes: Sounds reasonable to me.

Opening FHP Facilities to Non-FHP Members

Hughes: One of the things that happened with this restructuring was that FHP facilities were supposed to now be open to non-FHP members. Isn't that illegal? I thought that there was a state or a federal regulation that restricted FHP facilities to FHP members.

Gumbiner: Not if they become an independent medical group.

Hughes: Did non-FHP members use its services?

Gumbiner: I don't know who would walk in there except a deadbeat who did not pay the other doctors in the community. It is a good place to go--the FHP center, now the Talbert Medical Group. You can get in there and they will treat you for free.

You see, the whole idea of prepaid group practice is very simple. All members have to do is present an FHP card and they run it through the little machine and it tells you if they are a paid-up member. That's it. Bingo! They pay the three dollars or whatever it is, and they get all the service they need. It has already been paid for. You do not have to collect or worry about people not paying. And that is why FHP medical group culture is not going to be successful in fee-for-service. Fee-for-service is very complicated to make successful. They have to make sure everybody can pay and their insurance is good, that there is not a deductible or co-payment they should be paying, and so forth.

Medicine and Money

Hughes: Also, people like you, who combine medical training and business acumen, are a rare breed. The average physician is notorious for being a poor business manager.

Gumbiner: Physicians should not be in business. It is too complicated.

When I began to practice [1948], there was no medical insurance, if you can believe that. A patient walked into my office and I had to get paid to make a living. In other words, I had to keep training my front office personnel to say, "That will be X dollars." Not to say, "Would you like to pay?" Of course they wouldn't like to pay.

There are always people who say, "Well, Doc, I just went through personal bankruptcy. I guess that makes us even, and I can start coming back in again [for your medical services]." I said, "No, you can't." Then you have all of these horror stories about fee-for-service with people saying, "We are not delivering your baby here unless you pay first." But then a woman appears with the baby's head on the perineum; she has no money; they had to deliver her, right? And she never pays them.

I guess what I am talking about is I am not too sure that shareholders' return should be the major element that we address in a medical establishment. Perhaps managed care should be like a utility: the shareholder gets a certain return and that is it, period. They are not going to get 100 times their investment as with computer stocks. Health care should not be in that marketplace. There are too many ways you can squeeze it.

For instance, patients do not know what [care] they should get and what they should not get. They are depending upon the doctor to be the purchaser of care for them. And you do not want the doctor to be motivated by only financial interests. The shareholders' concept of the best return for themselves puts a squeeze on the providers, and these attitudes all filter down.

Hughes: If medicine turns into an investor-controlled profession, you are not going to get the same sort of person going into medicine.

Gumbiner: Well, the people going into medicine now do not know what is going on in reality. You have more applications for medical school positions now than you ever had. Maybe I should lecture to medical students. On the other hand, it's a dilemma. If you were to say, "We need a better system; we cannot go on with the old fee-for-service cottage industry--"

Hughes: Well, that's dead.

Gumbiner: Well, maybe it's dead, all right, but it is not that dead in some of these small towns in middle America. And then you say, "Well now, if that's true, we cannot go along with that. We have to have some type of organized or managed care." The whole idea is that the name "managed care" means you manage care.

Anderson is not interested in management; he wants to get rid of management. He fired most of the management. He is not interested in good health care, effective delivery of care, or growth and innovation. His main objective is to get rid of every full-time-equivalent employee he can. But if you do that you do not have management and you no longer have managed care. So it follows that to increase the shareholders' return, he is going to destroy management and work with as little management as possible. In order to increase the shareholders' return, you are going to take as much out of the provider's pocket as you can, resulting in poor morale and poor service.

I am not saying that we cannot take it out of the provider's pocket in the U.S.A., because we have the best-paid providers in the world. However, most people going into medical school now I think are going in for reasonably altruistic reasons, but I bet they feel that they will have a secure livelihood for the rest of their lives--they think. They may think wrong.

Interestingly enough, for the first time this year, the entering class at Harvard was over 50 percent women. Now, what that has to do with it is only left to conjecture, because I think that you get fewer working years out of a female doctor than a male doctor, because many women take off time to have children. Most of the women doctors I know have dropped out from time to time to take care of their kids or family. They have a tendency to go into less time-consuming specialties, like dermatology and ophthalmology, or to work for organizations that allow them regular hours or more time off. Perhaps they will be less financially demanding.

If you were to look into it and say, "What percentage of doctors today are care-givers?"

Hughes: What do you mean by that? Primary care?

Gumbiner: No, care-givers. Care-givers who want to give care to people. Well, of the doctors I know, maybe 20 percent at the most are true care-givers. The other 80 percent are what I call techno-scientists. They are in health care because it is scientific. The type of people that get into medical school make high grades in undergraduate school, right? These days you have to have a 3.5 to a 4.0 [grade point average] to get into a medical school. What kind of people are those? Are they the type that are well-rounded, that are out amongst the folks? Probably not.

Hughes: I take your point, but the current move towards primary-care specialists appears to counter that trend. My understanding is that there are state-mandated quotas--certainly in California--so that a medical school with state financial backing has a quota by department for how many specialists in a given field can be turned out. And the number is declining in non-primary care specialties. Yet a primary-care specialty may be encouraged to turn out twice the number of doctors.

Gumbiner: Well, this is all very philosophical and has to do with the problem of what role the investor-controlled HMO provider should pay. This could include hospital chains, some of which are buying medical schools; it could be HMOs buying medical schools; it could be a number of other entities. The question is, will the publicly traded HMOs contribute to the community by supporting education and research?

Hughes: How does a founder and long-term director make allowances for changes in history? The environment when you began this company in the early sixties is very different from that in the mid-nineties.

Gumbiner: We moved with the times and changed from a staff model to a mixed model with the majority of our business being in the IPA. I think the one thing that I did not count on was how the financial environment changed. The public HMOs are investor driven and not medical provider-driven. The environment had changed from the evolution of the socially conscious, achievement-oriented health plan into the money-driven, materialistic, short-sighted, greedy investor-oriented organization.

Now, that can happen in many other industries; you expect that in industries where profit is the driving motive. But you do not expect it in the HMO field, because there are still a lot of not-for-profit HMOs and people who are interested in the mission to deliver the most care to the most people for the least amount of money and to improve the quality and availability of health care.

Hughes: Were those the aims of the majority of FHP personnel?

Gumbiner: I think so. I do not think that the majority of people I hired were there just to see how much money they could make. We prided ourselves in having more care-givers amongst our providers than you find in the fee-for-service sector. As a whole, our people could concentrate on being care-givers because they did not have to worry about running an office or meeting their bills or all these other things that the fee-for-service doctors have to do.

Robert Gumbiner's Burnout and Ill Health [Interview 3: February 14, 1996]

Gumbiner: Let's talk about the emotional aspects of this takeover. This can include a burned-out or disinterested CEO/chairman who resents all of the work and hassles and the political maneuvering. This will show to the board of directors and staff.

On the other hand, if he or she is too successful and is dealing with board members that are not that successful in their own right, then you have jealousy and envy on their part that plays into it. How much it plays into it, no one knows. People do many things [for emotional or subconscious reasons]. They do not particularly do them on a logical basis. Why would my two long-time board members, for instance, decide that they would prefer to have leadership come from a company we acquired and paid a premium for and they knew nothing about? They could be the laughingstock of the industry. They had to have a reason. And the reason probably was not fully monetary, although they were rewarded handsomely with company money for their vote.

I think that the chairman has to pay attention to the emotional content of a situation where you may make people envious and jealous because you are too successful; you may make them angry because you are not paying attention to them or you don't seek or take their advice; or you may get them annoyed by perhaps coming to a meeting late. The chairman may be acting in a self-defeating manner in regard to the board and its support.

If you are a student of human behavior, you say, "Why would a chairman do that?" Somebody might do that because he did not want to be chairman any more and could not figure out how to leave gracefully. So he gets the job done by acting in such a way that his board members either become angry with him or hook up with someone else to get even.

I think when a founder/CEO retires, his major plan, thrust, and concentration should be on finding someone or a system or structure that will carry on the organization in the manner that made it successful, instead of just hoping that a successor will get the job done.

Hughes: I am wondering how much burnout was a factor in the case of Robert Gumbiner. You had been doing this for decades.

Gumbiner: That was a major factor. My message to people who find themselves in the same position is that they should have a definite plan and timing of how they are going to replace themselves. Do not just drift forever. The other thing that played a part was my surgery and problems that I had with prostate cancer.

Hughes: What you are saying is that surgery was a complication, but there were problems that predated that, namely, burnout and the fact that your life was no longer totally focused on the company.

Gumbiner: That's true. And I had other personal distractions. Nevertheless, I think that if the founder and CEO wants his vision to continue, he should make plans to make that happen.

Doctor-Managers

Hughes: What difference do you think it made that the people making the decisions, the executives (with the exception of you), were not M.D.s, and, I understand, there was no mechanism for physicians and the nursing staff to have a direct imprint on policy?

Gumbiner: That is not exactly true. We had been training doctor-managers for years, and some had important general management positions. One was in charge of [the program in] San Diego and another of Northern California. I think that the lack of more doctor-managers was a significant problem in senior management. Also, I did not recognize the lack of doctors in board of directors' representation. I was into the management theory that doctors practice medicine and managers manage, and that management would not try to practice medicine and doctors would not try to manage.

Somewhere along the line, I think there should have been more input by the providers. It could have saved the company and maintained the FHP mission which is, deliver care in a new, innovative, creative fashion on an economically sound basis. More expansion of management-trained doctors probably would have helped, but it is always a disaster to let management-naïve doctors take charge.

After this takeover and with the accent solely on shareholders' and investors' interests, the whole idea of delivering care to the most people for the least amount of money was totally obviated and scrambled to create more shareholders1 wealth. What you have to watch out for is the type of management people that you bring aboard. People you are going to attract to a for-profit public company can well be people who are more interested in increasing their own personal wealth than they are in building and achieving for the company.

Hughes: People from a business orientation don't necessarily understand medical philosophy. Whether they are looking for personal grandisement or not, the philosophies in business and medicine are different.

Gumbiner: I doubt that greed is limited to businessmen--there are plenty of greedy doctors. Self-centered, greedy people come from all fields and walks of life. Take the entertainment industry. Some of these folks are multi-multi-millionaires, even billionaires, and yet they work like dogs. For instance, Michael Eisner, who is head of Disney, is very, very wealthy. He had a triple cardiac bypass last year. But he is a workaholic. He is hyperactive, over-committed. Why would somebody do that? They are obviously not doing it for money. They have all the money they need. They are doing it for personal accomplishment and achievement and all of the perks they get, psychic income.

Hughes: What I was trying to get at is the clash of cultures: medical culture not being completely in sync with business culture.

Gumbiner: Well, let's put it another way. I do not think medical culture is necessarily altruistic, nor is business culture necessarily non-altruistic. You have businesses that are socially conscious in that they take care of their employees and produce a profit at the same time. There are doctors who are self-centered and focused on their own personal financial gain while at the same time attempting to be caregivers.

But I think there is a greater probability of profitability if you meld into management the right folks from the provider group. At least they understand what you are trying to do and the difficulty of trying to do it. You cannot have somebody manage the staff-model medical group that has never worked with patients. They do not have a clue of how and why systems work. If management says, "Well, we are going to increase the doctors' load from twenty-five patients a day to thirty-five," they do not understand if you do that to a doctor, he will just churn. In other words, he will have his old patients come back; he will introduce himself and establish rapport, find out what is wrong with them, send the sick ones off to another specialist, and just churn [his not-so-sick patients]. His dance card will look just fine; it will be all filled up, but not productively.

Hughes: Isn't that a danger with the way health care is going?

Gumbiner: If you leave it totally up to the doctors or the providers, you have a good chance of not getting much productivity. Doctors are notoriously poor managers and not visionaries. Take the Swedish system for example: Several years ago, they managed to get the Swedish doctors to all agree to work for the federal government in return for extra time off and postgraduate time. Well, the last time I talked to the Swedish planners, they were complaining that they cannot get productivity out of the doctors. How are you going to get productivity from people who are only working about nine months out of the year?

I learned long ago that you can't have a psychiatrist or psychiatric social worker making their own appointments when they are working for a salary. They will make appointments with people that are not very difficult cases. They can sit there and schmooze with them. But just try to get them to do two group sessions a day. With some exceptions, they do not want to do that. They want to sit down and play Dr. Freud one-to-one and take a nap.

One time I had the doctors making their own appointments. Well, they would arrange for no appointments after four o'clock in the afternoon, or they would say, "All of my cases are very hard," so they would only see two patients in an hour. One guy was in the back playing chess with himself with an automatic chess set. You have those situations! We had a dentist in Guam whom we had to let go, because if he had a cancellation he would take a nap instead of helping out other dentists whose schedules were overloaded.

I do not think one can be simplistic and say the answer is having the providers run things. But I think the answer certainly is not in having financial people totally in charge.

Hughes: What about a mechanism for these two groups to communicate on a regular and organized basis?

Gumbiner: Unfortunately, some of the management people are ruthless and more confrontational than the doctors, and they will intimidate the doctors by firing a few, like they did in this situation [with Talbert Medical Group]. They say, "Well, we want you to sign contracts with us as independent operators, and if you don't, we will fire you." These doctors say, "Wait a minute, if I get fired,

I can't pay my mortgage." If they were confrontational, they would have formed a union and fought back, but they were not.

Probably one of my problems was that I was still a little naive and not ruthless enough, or I would have gotten rid of some of these troublemakers. If you kill the baby, it's not going to grow up to stab you.

The $23 Million Mistake

Hughes: I read of a $23 million mistake in California. What is that?

Gumbiner: Well, I wasn't too aware-of that, because they tried to hide it. But they had a $23 million mistake in the way they handled something, and it appeared on the books in error as a charge against earnings. It really was in this guy Judd Jessup's shop, but he managed to spin it off and claim it was the problem of one of the FHP managers.

They, meaning Anderson, were attempting to fire as many FHP managers as they could. He said, "Oh, this woman has been working for us for sixteen or seventeen years. She made a big mistake here. I guess we will have to relieve her from her responsibilities. Anybody have an objection?" That's the way he worked. Burke [Gumbiner] said, "The chairman can't fire an employee who reports to someone else." So Anderson called in this guy Jessup--his stooge--and had him fire her. She claims that [the financial loss] wasn't her mistake.

Hughes: And that was the end of that?

Gumbiner: She's out! She was going to sue them for wrongful dismissal, but she ran out of money to pay attorneys.

The Need for Hospitals

Hughes: You said yesterday that it was erroneous to think that the majority of the board of directors should be outsiders.

Gumbiner: That's right. Even if the so-called outsiders look good on paper and they give you unbiased, objective opinions based on their experience in management, they still don't know the [HMO] industry. In other words, if you look at the numbers that Anderson and his gang [came up with], you see that the hospitals are not making the return that a similar investment could make in the IPA, so you would come to the conclusion to sell the hospitals. On the other hand, they do not realize that the hospitals and the staff models are what every IPA operator would love to have because they could keep them competitive.

It's like insurance; your insurance premiums do not make money, but you pay the malpractice premiums anyhow. In the year 2010 we are going to have 60 million Medicare people, not 37 million as we have today, and we have not built too many hospital beds in this country in the last twenty years. These extra 30 million people are not going to use just four times but probably six times the care that younger people use, because they are not just over sixty-five but in their eighties. They will be sicker and use more Medicare, and you will run out of hospital beds. If you do not have any hospital beds, the IPA cannot operate, because now they have to pay whatever the hospitals want to charge them, because the hospital will not make contracts with them- they are full.

The other thing they do not know is that I would say 50 percent of the hospitals in this country are obsolete. They have been around for fifty years and they should be replaced. They should be torn down and turned into something else, and new acute hospitals should be built. The acute hospital of the future will have mostly intensive-care beds and backed up by sub-acute hospitals. Sub-acute hospitals are a lot less expensive and you do not have to carry the burden of x-ray equipment, special procedure equipment, laboratory equipment, et cetera. All you are doing is supplying somebody in a bed with nursing care. The difference is the difference between a $1,100 to $1,500-a-day hospital bed in an acute hospital today and a $250-a-day hospital bed.

These people who took over FHP closed our sub-acute hospital, which was a concept that we had that was saving us a lot of money. Now it is going to cost them more money for hospital care, but they do not understand this! They say, "We've got extra beds in our acute hospital, so why should we have a sub-acute hospital? We will close it. We will put people in the acute hospital beds." Well, according to the marginal utility of money theory, for the acute hospital bed, that's true. If you have an empty bed and you stick somebody in there, you are just going to pay for their room and board. But sooner or later, those beds fill up. Now you are short. Now you have to find a place for these people. And you do not have your sub-acute hospital. So the HMO pays a premium for intensive-care beds where FHP doctors do not have staff privileges and have no control over treatment or costs. It's all a problem of short range thinking against long-range thinking.

Hughes: Not just FHP hospitals but a lot of hospitals have empty beds. How does a company get past this present rough period where it can't fill up the beds?

Gumbiner: Well, you would never open up a hospital for an HMO with the idea that the beds would be full, because then you could not grow. You would have to build another hospital. I anticipated that we would build when our beds were 50 percent full. That was the whole idea: we would have a chance to grow and plan. Now, if you owned a standard fee-for-service hospital, you would want to fill all of the beds. But if a hospital is part of a managed care delivery system, what you want to do is give yourself a margin for growth, particularly if you are bringing in more Medicare patients, which use a lot more hospital care. Besides, the HMO is paid for hospital care whether it is used or not.

Hughes: And then you put your effort into growing.

Gumbiner: That is exactly what should have been done. The energy and time and money should have been put into marketing and growing, particularly in the Medicare section in Northern California. But that did not happen because of the change in philosophy. FHP's new management is not interested in growing; it is interested in dismembering the company and selling the carcass. When you cut out staff, you can not grow; it prohibits you from growing.

Hughes: Some believe that with the trend towards cost-cutting and retrenchment, the incentive for growth is being lost.

Gumbiner: Exactly--growth, achievement, fun, excitement, getting up and going to work in the morning and enjoying it. If you go to work in the morning and you are just tapping sand in a rat hole and you could be fired in the next wave, if you are any good, you start looking for another job. And if you are not, you are terrorized and you do not get anything done.

IPAs

Hughes: Ed Keaney, who is an analyst at the investment banker and brokerage firm of Volpe, Welty and Company, has been quoted several times in articles concerning FHP. He said that the staff model in the sixties and seventies allowed health plan executives to better control costs by owning hospitals and employing M.D.s. Then he says, "But in the nineties, the information technology has advanced to the point that health plans are able to exert a great deal of control over the behavior of physicians and hospitals without having to own them. I don't think Dr. Gumbiner is fully in recognition of that."24

Gumbiner: Not true. First of all he is no expert in health care management; he is just a financial analyst. If you run your lifestyle on the advice of an investment broker you will be in deep trouble. He is just wrong!

IPAs can control the behavior of hospitals as far as getting more favorable financial contracts for hospitals, but they are still not able to control the ambience, the physical plant, the bad emergency room, the bad food, the quality of care in general. And innovation--forget it!

We have threatened hospitals by removing people unless they make the food better or have a better emergency room and keep the place clean. They say, "Yes, we will do it." They do not have the ability to do it. That is the bottom line. They do not have the skilled management. They do not have the focus.

Hospital administrators are notoriously poor managers, with a few exceptions, particularly in the not-for-profit field. What this analyst does not recognize is that you have to control all elements of a managed-care program in order to be successful, and if you don't, you cannot control it.

The End of Robert Gumbiner's Vision for FHP

Hughes: I think that a good place to end this long discussion would be your resolution about how to handle what you see as the destruction of your vision of FHP.

Gumbiner: I don't know if "handle" is the right term. I think that my advice to anybody else that this should happen to is: if you are going to do something about a takeover like this, you have to do it within about ninety days from the time it occurs. You can not let it go on for six months or a year. After that time, all you are going to regain if you take back control is a corpse. These takeover people only want to liquidate and are having a fire sale to destroy this company as fast as they can, so that somebody like myself could not come back in and recapture and rebuild it. I think that after six months to a year, no one can rescue it.

In my particular instance, my health was such that I felt that I could not mount a proxy fight or an attack within ninety days, which I would normally have done. One thing that gets my interest is a good fight, especially if I am on the side of right. I think that one has to try to figure out what your opponents' capacities are and what the cost will be in time, company and brought it back to growth and greatness, getting rid of the people who were causing the problems, and replaced them with competent people who were achievement-oriented rather than predators bent on destruction and personal gain. However, I do not think you can do much about it after time has gone by.

Having said that, you do not have to let them get away with theft. In other words, I do not really have to let them get away with stealing part of this medical group from the shareholders. That is just wrong, management giving themselves 10 percent of the shareholders1 $400 million assets for no investment.

Current Interests

Gumbiner: I think I will probably have to concentrate my life on recovering my health. Once I do that, I will probably go off in a different direction. Right now I am working on opening a Latin American museum of art.25 In addition, I am doing a philanthropic program in health care for low-income people in Santa Ana.

Hughes: Do you want to expand a little on Santa Ana?

Gumbiner: I started the Santa Ana project when I was chairman of the FHP Foundation. It is an idea that is patterned somewhat after our Outer Island Dispensary System in Yap, that is, three to five very small medical centers that we can man with mid-level medical providers reporting to one physician. This would remove the barriers between the low-income person and the person providing health care because it is free, available, and accessible. They are really health centers, not clinics, because our emphasis is on preventive care: immunization and well-baby care, family planning, maternal health. We will be doing stopgap medicine for people who have problems and also will act as an ombudsman until we find them a doctor and a hospital bed. You have to bring health care to the population; you cannot expect people to find their way into a sophisticated hospital or a distant clinic site. They do not have transportation and they do not know what is available or that they should seek help.

Hughes: How is that program underwritten?

Gumbiner: The foundation is underwriting it for about $1.5 million a year for three years. The trick is to watch your dollars and get maximum value.

Hughes: Are you overseeing that project?

Gumbiner: I am the chairman, but I have an executive director who is doing the day-to-day work. I am just there to give it some stimulus, guidance, and policy direction. It's not something I want to do because I would rather move completely out of the health care field for a while.

Hughes: When did you make the decision to get out of health care?

Gumbiner: It is something I have thought about recently. I think that I have been in health care too long, and given the circumstances of the last year or two, I think I would be better off in another field. It would be more interesting. Besides, there is too much money on the table in managed care today. This makes people act strangely and attracts the wrong people with the wrong motives into the field. I think the creative, fun cycle is about over. In the future I will only work with people I like. My feeling is if you can't have fun in whatever you are doing, whether it is organizational development, planning or operations, then you should not get out of bed in the morning.

My regrets are that I am not able to bring the medical school concept into the HMO. No more accusing HMOs of second rate doctors. This would have been the ultimate marketing project, the totally integrated health care system, from the training of doctors and other individual professionals, to the organization and delivery of preventative and corrective care, as well as the maintenance of physical, mental, and social well being.

Hughes: Is that it?
Gumbiner: Yes!

Hughes: Thank you.

EPILOGUE 1
WHAT HAPPENED AFTER I
RESIGNED FROM FHP

January 1997

The first book I wrote in 1977 was called *"The HMO, Putting It All Together"*. This epilog of what happened after I resigned from the FHP Board of Directors, could be called *"The HMO, Taking It All Apart"*.

After the FHP Board of Directors meeting at which the Board voted to replace me with Jack Anderson as chairman and to make me chairman emeritus, I realized that I could not work with the likes of Jack Anderson. I surmised that future board meetings would be nothing but continual arguments as I attempted to keep him from destroying the company. Somehow Jack Anderson had seduced two of my Board members, so along with himself and his crony, he was able to control the seven person board. My attending physicians' advice was to resign since I was on continual antibiotic therapy following my surgery and the continuing stress was impairing my immune system. Therefore I made a decision to resign from the FHP Board, put that behind me, and attempt to get well.

With no opposition, Jack Anderson, who was essentially an insurance executive and investor, began the immediate dismantling of FHP International. His first move was to give Price his marching orders to sell the FHP acute hospitals and sell the FHP sub-acute hospitals. The hospitals were sold in a short time at a discount. Three decades of careful building an integrated health care system was destroyed in three months. The Orange County, Fountain Valley Hospital sold to Memorial Hospital in Long Beach and the Utah Hospital sold to the Paracelsus Hospital Corporation.

As an aside, both of these hospital companies immediately got into trouble. Memorial Hospital in Long Beach ended up in arbitration attempting to get some $280 million back from FHP. They alleged that the number of patients that FHP would put in this hospital and the income generated was misrepresented to them and that they would lose $280 million over the next ten years. Paracelsus Hospital got into so much financial trouble that they were forced to close three of their other hospitals. The Utah State Health Department shut down the emergency room of the former FHP Hospital for a period of thirty hours because it was undermanned.

The next move Anderson made was to instruct Price to fire most of the FHP senior management. These included Chris Selecky who was in charge of California IPAs, Tim Brady who was in charge of the Riverside Division, and Ryan Trimble who was in charge of the FHP Staff Models in California. He even stooped to closing the art galleries; the one in Long Beach and the new gallery in Utah, saving a measly $300,000 a year and wrecking that P.R. program. Judd Jessup, who had been CEO of TakeCare, was put in charge of the FHP IPA division. On Anderson's marching orders Jessup fired so many FHP senior management people that he ended up having some 24-25 people reporting directly to him. This, of course, was an impossible management situation and Jessup began failing miserably; resigning shortly thereafter.

Anderson's tactics of terminating the senior management were completely in opposition to any good management concept of how to build a company. J. Pierpont Morgan years ago said, "Take away my ships and my factories and my banks but let me keep my management and I will have everything back again." Anderson went exactly the other way. He cut the head off of the organization. There was no direction and no management; he focused only on squeezing every last dollar out of the organization in order to make the bottom line look better short term so he could sell what was left at the highest price.

He then added two more of his cronies and one of Joe Prevratil's to the Board of Directors. This so frightened W.W. Price Ill, the so-called CEO, that he continued to follow Anderson's direction to keep his job for a few more months and become even more of a cipher.

The next thing that happened was to spin off the Staff Model, alleging that the Staff Model wasn't making money and therefore it wasn't worth anything. The Staff Model had a gross revenue income of over $400 million a year; it owned or leased over fifty medical centers, fully staffed and equipped. By anybody's calculation who knows anything, this operation was worth over $400 million. The alleged costs against that gross income was suspect for several reasons. Anderson managed to spin it off with the help of the Board of Directors into an independent organization for a projected sale of $60 Million. The idea was that this medical division would then get patients from other HMOs as an independent medical group and be successful. How he thought that a streamlined staff model could be more successful as an old fashioned medical group than a staff model, is beyond me.

In a rather complicated scheme, he arranged to have FHP sustain this Staff Model for about a year by paying an inflated capitation rate for each enrollee. The idea being that the management organization would receive about 10 percent of the value of the medical group, i.e. they would pay $9,600 for 10 percent of this $400 million asset. Then the medical group would buy itself from PacifiCare for $60 million. They would get the $60 million by floating 60 million shares and selling the rights to each share for one dollar a piece. They would use this money then to buy this $400 million asset from PacifiCare for $60 million. At of this writing, it is not known whether this scheme will be successful or not. To make it more confusing, they did a reverse split, dividing the total shares by 21.50, making the shares worth $21.50 each.

Then PacifiCare decided in negotiating rates with this independent medical group that they would not pay the subsidized rates, rather they would pay the regular rates. Therefore this organization became short cash-wise. They have already admitted to losing $9 million last year. The story they give, however, is that this loss is really the result of the losses of the Staff Model beforehand, which of course is baloney. Probably, they will prepay some 1997 costs in 1996 to make 1997 look better; i.e., "dress it up for sale". This is only one of the items that makes their cost side of the balance sheet suspect.

The other interesting thing, is that these other HMOs, although they may contract with FHP, are not going to produce enrollees because the competition (the other medical groups and doctors), are going to hang onto their patients and not let them go to this new medical group. Time will tell how this works out.

After selling the hospitals at a discount and everything else that he could get his hands on including the FHP airplane, all of the land that had been acquired and land banked for future development, Anderson set out to sell what was left of FHP to another HMO.

When I left FHP it was a vibrant, successful organization with some $600 million in cash plus land in several states that had been researched and purchased for future expansions, and very little debt. For instance, there were 11 acres purchased off of a freeway in Albuquerque, New Mexico; there were 21 acres off a freeway in Phoenix, Arizona; there were 7 acres in Riverside. My concept had been that you buy land when you can get it, when it is inexpensive, and you hold it and you use it to build your centers and your hospitals when you need it. The fact that you have the land and you have a sign on it, "Future Home Of ..." has a tendency to calm down the IPA doctors. Anderson does not understand this, he never understood it and he never understood much about the HMO business.

FHP was then head and shoulders above the other HMOs because of the mixed model concept- that is, going in with the quick marketing contract IPA and then backing it up for competitive control and capacity where doctors didn't exist with the Staff Model. The Mayo Clinic is now imitating our mixed model in Arizona.

The problem with the contract HMOs is that the organization can only contract with the doctors and hospitals that are there. If the hospitals are not very good, that's what you have. If the doctors are not very good, that's what you have. And if the doctors are not there in the adequate numbers of primary care and the specialties are needed, that's what you have; you don't have a managed care system. However, with the mixed model we had the ability to bring in staff models and if we needed two orthopedists we would bring them in, if we needed five general practitioners in a certain area we would bring those in, etc. We had the strength to upgrade the hospitals we used and if they wouldn't do that we would build our own hospitals or threaten to build them. Since FHP had built hospitals they knew we could do this and they would upgrade. This concept was never recognized by Anderson or our other two board members.

You might say that the FHP direction under my guidance of innovation, controlled growth, independent economic viability, development of management staff in depth, quality image and controlled flexibility was totally missing in his concept. He went so far as to tell people directly that he was only interested in maximizing shareholders' income.

At the time of this writing, several things are about to happen. This is January of 1997. PacifiCare has offered to buy what is left of FHP for $35 a share which is $17 in cash and the rest in PacifiCare "B" non-voting shares. Jack Anderson has notified all of the Senior Management of FHP that they are out; they will not be retained. The insurance division is being folded into Pacificare's insurance division.

Jack Anderson and Joe Prevratil have been elected to sit on the PacifiCare Board of Directors. These are the two engineers of the takeover of FHP. This is like injecting yourself with the Ebola virus for PacifiCare. PacifiCare has reorganized their board and enlarged it to twelve where they have six people from UniHealth, which is their parent, and six other people (two of which are these two treacherous connivers from FHP). They have gotten past the FTC where somebody had alleged that they were cornering the market on Medicare in San Diego. The SEC seems to not be making any noises and they are now waiting for the DOC (Department of Corporations) to approve this transaction and consumers groups are complaining.

The spun off medical group Talbert has flown a Red Herring, an S1, where they are attempting to go public so they can try to sell that company for $200 million or more. That's the company that they allegedly bought from FHP/PacifiCare for $96 million because it was worthless. In addition, Anderson and his buddies have the nerve to put themselves on the Board of Talbert and given themselves stock options, every single one of them, with the exception of Burke Gumbiner, who was left off of the Talbert Board, putting Jack Massimino in his place. Obviously they are just playing Burke along for a little cosmetic subterfuge.

Interesting, Anderson has already implied to the FHP Board members how he will take over the PacifiCare Board. First he says it is unfair for the PacifiCare people to have "B" non-voting stock and it should be turned into "A" stock. This will dilute the UniHealth holdings and control. PacifiCare now holds about 40 percent of the stock through UniHealth, their parent company. He also said it is not fair for UniHealth to have six members on the twelve member board when they only own 40 percent of the voting shares. (They will own less than 40 percent of voting shares if he gets rid of the "B" stock and converts it to "A".)

You can see the writing on the wall. He gets the UniHealth block down to about three to four out of the twelve, then he turns a couple more people his way, and he has seven, and he takes over PacifiCare. PacifiCare has done a few things right because they terminated what was left of TakeCare and FHP's Senior Management. But the question is, do they have enough management to run the larger company successfully?

In any event, what ended up as a proud, wonderful company that was FHP, with the objective to give the most health care to the most people for the least amount of money, projecting quality care in a managed health care system, has been obliterated. This was done by a greedy raider in cooperation with a few stupid board members who acted upon their emotions and greed rather than intellect. To people like Joe Prevratil, who is desperate and at the point of this reading is $6 million in debt in his Queen Mary operation, it is an attempt to save himself and he doesn't care how. To Anderson it is just a game to see how much money he can pile up on top of what he has and how many people he can screw.

Let this be a warning to other people in the HMO field on what can happen to them if they don't keep focusing on their business of providing health care and on succession with strong and determined managers. If they get the wrong people on the board who don't share their vision, and if they don't investigate thoroughly who they are getting in bed with.

This was a classic textbook example of a corporate raid. This is where an outsider gets control of the board, sells off everything that isn't nailed down to make the bottom line look better. They sell the component parts and then the carcass to somebody else, destroying the company.

It wasn't a raid on a company that was faltering, it was a company that was in good financial shape. The only thing that was faltering about it was the leadership by the CEO. There is a lesson to be learned by others and that is, you can't do something halfway and you have to be ruthless and leave like minded people and strong succession in charge.

EPILOGUE 2

June 2008

After the take over of FHP, the medical centers in Tucson, Phoenix, New Mexico and Las Vegas were all sold or abandoned. Guam was continued and turned into a routine medical group, no longer an HMO providing the best service on Guam. The hospital in Hawaiian Gardens was closed, the two sub-acute hospitals were sold. Our major hospital in Fountain Valley was sold to Memorial Hospital of Long Beach at a huge discount and our new hospital in Salt Lake City was sold to a foreign hospital investor and eventually was closed when it went bankrupt. Both legislative offices, one in Washington, D.C. and one in Sacramento, CA were closed, thus blinding FHP to legislative development.

Joe Prevratil continued to run the Queen Mary. I eventually got one of the two million dollars back that I had invested in the boat through litigation by giving this one million dollar note to MoLAA, the Museum of Latin American Art. Mr. Prevratil ended up bankrupting the boat and being sued by the City of Long Beach.

What were the remains of FHP was acquired for pennies on the dollar by PacifiCare. PacifiCare was eventually acquired by United Health Care. United had a scandal and had to fire their CEO for stock manipulation but carries on and is now losing money.

So the whole staff model FHP HMO was erased, the senior management was all fired, the medical group was sold to a group from Alabama, which eventually got into trouble, went bankrupt and had to sell it back. The group in Long Beach, California was taken over by the doctors, but the other states just disappeared. The FHP membership was eventually sold to PacifiCare, then to United Health, when they became just another health and accident insurance company, calling themselves an HMO.

However, our concept was sound. FHP was financially secure, it was successful. It had little if any debt. It had been generating cash for expansion. It was well managed with a great staff of physicians. In the end it was a lack of a successful back-up plan (or succession plan 2 and 3), that did FHP in. I mistakenly thought that one succession plan would do it when, of course, it didn't do so because the first succession plan usually fails.

But I must take full responsibility for the success and the failure of FHP, whether it was sub-conscious or not. This great experiment of seamless managed care came to a disastrous end. I am still thoroughly convinced that the most efficient, cost contained quality care can be given through a team of staff models HMOs where the hospital, prescription drugs, mental health, ambulance service, dental, eye care, all come through one source with the savings that are engendered through this type of matrix managed care.

Today the only really true HMO is Kaiser Permanente. The rest of the so-called HMOs have been gobbled up by the insurance companies and what are now called "HMOs" are simply insurance companies that are using a different type of payment for the providers. They save money for themselves on the providers' side but with no concern about the availability, or the accessibility- the basic HMO concept.

The current USA disorganized health care delivery system continues to be under-staffed geographically and by specialty. Waste and fraud are rampant under the obsolete fee-for-service system. The USA public pays more and gets less in health care value than any other first world country.

Meanwhile, the cost of health care continues to rise dramatically while health insurance continues to cover less and less of the cost.

APPENDIX A -

TAKING APART THE HMO
FHP CHRONOLOGY

June 26, 1995	Mass firing begins
June 26, 1995	FHP Hospitals offered for sale
June 26, 1995	Medical group spin-off
June 26, 1995	Special Board of Directors meeting takes place; restructuring begins
June 22, 1995	Robert Gumbiner resigns
June 15, 1995	Jack Anderson becomes Chairman of FHP Board of Directors, Robert Gumbiner becomes Chairman Emeritus (special Board of Directors meeting set for restructure)
May 30, 1995	Robert Gumbiner 2nd prostate surgery
March 9, 1995	Board of Directors meeting, Utah (RG unable to attend because of illness)
February 24, 1995	Jack Anderson calls special Board meeting
February 8, 1995	Robert Gumbiner first prostatic surgery

NOTE:	Something should have been done July-Aug. 1994, i.e. b/d election
June 30, 1994	Richard Rodnick resigns from the Board (Board reduced from 9 to 8) One vacancy
June 24, 1994	FHP Board of Directors' seats enlarged from no less than 7 to no more than 11. Executive Meeting: June 28, 1994
June 17, 1994	TakeCare acquisition deal closes
October, 1993	FHP Office of the President established (to go for 2 years)

APPENDIX B -

MY ADVICE TO FOUNDERS & CHAIRMEN

WHO WISH TO RETIRE FROM THE DAY TO DAY ACTIVITES OF THE COMPANY BUT HAVE A DESIRE TO LEAVE THE COMPANY HEADED ALONG THE SAME PATH AS THEIR ORIGINAL STRATEGY

By Robert Gumbiner, M.D.
Founder, Former CEO and Former Chairman of FHP, Inc.

March 1996

The biggest breakthrough that FHP made is when we created and took on the MediCal (Medicaid) prepayment contract for the state of California when everybody else, including Kaiser, considered this not the thing to do. Steadfast adherence to the benefits and advantages to the company of MediCare risk contracts, i.e. prepayment contracts from the Federal Government for MediCare, was derided by Wall Street and all of the other HMOs.

A lesson to be learned here is that you cannot take the advice of others or become intimidated by them! You have to run your company in the best interest of the company, long term and do it with vision. Since Wall Street has no vision, a public company should not take the analysis or fund manager's advice on how to run the company since their vision extends to the end of the next quarter. Any management that tries to dance to the Wall Street tune instead of taking an objective viewpoint of what was best for the company and the industry will not move forward long term.

The problem for the Chief Executive and the Founder moving up to Chairman is that they do it because they want to discontinue expending the energy and time it takes to run the company. To be successful, and they must have a dedicated staff that reports only to them and to the Board of Directors. They must not depend upon receiving information through the management. New management, by its very nature, may attempt to put their "own paw print" on the company. Some people are just waiting for the CEO to move aside to they can run things differently. Never mind that their ambition exceeds their ability. It's just that they want to do it differently even though the way that it has been done has been successful.

The first move is for the Chairman to create an independent staff. In other words, he should have a secretary, a legal assistant for governance, and a financial officer who reports only to him and he should have a couple of assistants to get him information.

Most importantly, with any major policy decision such as acquisitions, the Chairman is going to have to come back into the picture and negotiate directly with the Chairman and the CEO of the other organization. He can not leave it up to his own management people.

A mistake made by FHP that should have been taken care of at the very beginning when negotiations looked like they were opening up, was that the Board and the Chairman should have gotten an <u>independent consultant</u> to review this transaction and give us advice of whether this was a reasonable transaction or not. Instead, we were getting all of our information through Bill Price, who was being manipulated by the underwriters, who wanted their 6 percent on the deal. The higher the price, the better for them They kept coming back with a higher price, telling Price and proving to him with the manipulated numbers, that it was a good price and everything was fine and dandy. Everything was not fine and dandy! Price knew that I wasn't too delighted with this deal. I though we were paying too much and acquiring too much debt.

In December of 1994, after we had rejected this deal at $62 a share, I was assured by Price and Hacken that the deal would not go forward and nothing would happen for 60 days. I left the country for three weeks on vacation over Christmas. Price then stepped up the activity to try to finalize this while I was gone. Price had several meetings with Anderson that I knew nothing of. Then all of a sudden the Board of Directors wanted to close a letter of intent or a preliminary agreement without sufficient investigation and due diligence. l was out of the country and they even went as far as fly the whole Board to Singapore, to meet with me, to try to make this happen. I later found out that there was an FHP management due diligence committee but I was kept in the dark.

Personally, I don't really know what went on behind my back between Price, Hacken and Anderson. I think the whole thing was being moved by the investment bankers.

Perhaps the fact that I really didn't want to pay any attention to it was because I was tired and bored with the whole thing. I probably subconsciously wanted to get out.

A major mistake here was in not figuring out what Anderson's goals were. In other words, he should have been asked the questions point blank, "do you want to grow this company or do want to sell this company?" Most importantly there should have been a private investigative company that investigated Mr. Anderson and Mr. Burdge, i.e. what they had done in the past in acquisitions and management. In the little that I know about Jack Anderson, he had been a Cigna executive and took over the Arizona Health Plan and then proceeded to wreck it. Cigna, at the time he was involved, was the laughing stock of the entire industry. He also acquired the two sickest companies in the industry, which were Ross Loos and HOMI. Never put somebody on a Board of Directors who is philosophically different than the person who built the company! Basic concept- two merging companies must have similar cultures.

As an aside, what happens gradually in a public company is that you find yourself surrounded by small-minded, short-term thinkers who are "high in the greed poll" and "low on the altruistic scale". This is because many times the people that join public companies join them and work in them mainly to increase their personal wealth and not to achieve something for society or for the industry.

In an acquisition like this; (1) there should be an independent consultant to the Chairman and the Board on the pluses and minuses of the deal, (2) there should be independent legal counsel for the Chairman and the Board, (3) there should be a formal investigation of the background and the history of the people you are dealing with, and (4) you should interview some of the management people of the target company just as if you are hiring them, and get a background history on the management people and their achievement in the company.

Most importantly, what is the philosophy of the company and the people that are working in it, and the Chairman and the Chief Executive Officer? Is the Chairman really acting as the CEO or do they really have a Chief Executive Officer?

The solution to keeping a company going in the right direction and with the right policy after the founder and CEO retires and becomes Chairman, is to make sure that the people that follow are thinking along the lines that made the company great. What are their cultural values? Don't fall for the idea that the original premises were obsolete and now the company should be changed, and become a follower rather than a leader.

Therefore it would be my advice to take your number two man and put him in that slot, which seems the obvious thing to do. But I would make a definite trial period of one year to eighteen months, with firm goals, evaluations of how he selects his staff, how he sets up his tables of organization, what is his vision, how he does marketing, etc. If he doesn't hit the 80 to 90 percentile on this, you simply terminate him, that's all, while you have the power. Then go out and recruit the next best person you can, either inside or outside, and give them the one year to eighteen months.

The question then is, will they accept the corporate goals or are they just waiting to push you aside when you turn your back so they can put their paw print on things and change things all around? The way they try it is little by little-- they will try one thing and if they get away with that, then they will try another. They become embolden as they go along. If the Chairman does not pay attention and does not focus on this and he wants to just be a traditional, non-executive Chairman, he is headed for serious trouble.

The executive chairman is a position that still retains power over the strategic direction of the company, the approval and negotiation of any mergers or acquisitions, significantly innovative changes and the corporate culture. The traditional chairman merely conducts the board of directors meetings and acts as a conduit for information between the board and management. The problem with the traditional chairman model is that the chairman has no way to obtain valid information to formulate decisions and eventually becomes a figurehead.

In my opinion the position of the traditional chairman should not exist since it becomes merely a place holder and it is subject to manipulation by management. To operate as an executive chairman an individual must have their own staff, subject to his hire and termination. This should include an assistant, a secretary, a legal resource and a financial analyst. This model allows the chair to obtain independent information and avoids the problem of isolation, misinformation and secret plotting within management.

You are either in or you are out. Accept the responsibility and function of the executive chairman or leave, resign and sever relations with the company. Otherwise you will be responsible and get the blame anyway.

As to mergers and acquisitions, everyone knows that matching cultures are the only chance of success. Yet, organizations continue attempts to beat the odds and acquire or merge within opposing cultures. This is why over 50% of mergers and acquisitions fail. Unrealistic expectations will doom an acquisition.

In the case of FHP acquiring TakeCare, the cultures could not be more dissimilar. TakeCare put the interest of the shareholder or investor first while FHP emphasized the interest of the patient and staff. TakeCare was in business for the short term and FHP for the long term. This should have been a deal killer from the beginning. The idea that by eliminating the TakeCare management somehow their culture could be changed was a mistake. A corporate culture permeates throughout the organization since only the individuals who believe in that culture will join and stay with the organization.

While FHP fostered innovation, staff development and marketing, TakeCare emphasized shareholders' profits. This strategy was incompatible.

When FHP acquired Utah Group Healthcare the objectives were closer and adaptable. Utah Group Health focused only on patient care mostly to the poor while FHP targeted patient care, organizational development and generating income to make it happen– a close fit.

I would advise the Chairman to get a Board of at least fifteen to twenty people; which is more difficult to manipulate than a board of seven or eight. Also, pick people that view things the way he or she does. In our case, we should have had about three or four doctors on the Board that believed in the Staff Model and HMO, with social consciousness. That would have worked. It is very important that, as Board people disappear, we appoint people that are on the right track philosophically; pruned out the people who were on the wrong track philosophically, and not worried about how competent they were as a Board Member.

My feeling is that the <u>Board Members should not own stock</u>, they should simply be paid a reasonable amount for their time. If they own stock, even a small amount, it may start short-range thinking, i.e. stock price.

I believe at least half of the people on the Board should be familiar with the industry, or at least providers; and the other half should be managers. But you should make sure they are really managers, i.e. Chief Executive Officers that were successful, with accent on "successful", and they should be from the service industry.

The question is, how do you keep the Board focused? Do you have people from the industry, people from outside the industry, do you have insiders, do you have outsiders or what do you have?

There must be a way to prevent a radical deviation from culture and policy, such as what has happened with FHP, where they sold off their best assets just for a perceived short-term stock market profit.

Succession really is the most important job of that retiring CEO as Chairman. That should be his main job, concentrating on that and on nothing else; i.e. evaluating the new CEO. For that purpose it is necessary that he continue to romance his Board of Directors. If they feel he is not focused and disinterested, they will begin power plays. If he is very successful, they may be envious and resentful anyhow. If you are egotistical and aloof, they will try to get you one way or the other. Finally, you have to like and respect them.

Envy, jealousy, greed and hate-- The Four Horseman ride within the Board of Directors.

This was written as advice to people that are in my position because what happen to me could happen to anybody. I wish somebody had given me this advice twelve years ago.

APPENDIX C -

THE STORY OF THE FHP FOUNDATION

October, 2008

The FHP Foundation was the outgrowth of the conversion of FHP from a non-profit to a for-profit organization. Effectively we purchased the non-profit from the state of California for $60 million after a long negotiation. The FHP for-profit, which eventually became public, had the obligation to pay off the $60 million to the State of California. In the negotiation it was agreed that the for-profit FHP would contribute $60 Million of stock from the public offering to a new non-profit foundation. This allowed that foundation to give away approximately $3 million a year. Part of this agreement was that the Foundation grants would go to the geographic areas where the money had been earned by the FHP non-profit and at least 50 percent would go to providing health care to the poor.

The challenge was to get grant requests that significantly fulfilled this obligation. We soon found out that just getting grants that came in voluntarily did not fit the obligations, purpose and strategy to provide care to the poor in the areas that this money had been earned.

The other challenge was getting a decent manager for this foundation. At that time the non-profit field was not too popular and most of the management types who had graduated with MBA's or had some management ability wanted to get into the for-profit financial field. So we had the problem of inadequate management resources.

Our board of directors did not know too much about health care but we were able to get a distinguished board of directors consisting of the President of the California State University at Long Beach, the President of the University of California at Irvine, the former Governor of Utah, the Long Beach City Manager, the President of FHP and myself. Part of the agreement was that FHP could not control this foundation but they were entitled to two seats on the nine person board. It became evident that we would have to create our own request for proposals (RFP's), but even that was difficult. For instance, when we set up a request for a proposal for $200,000 to use modern techniques of communication, advertising for health education we received only three that were appropriate.

We did some projects such as setting up a conference on "Who Cares for the Care Givers" and hosting the International Technological Assessment Association in a conference on evaluating new drug procedures and equipment. But we still had a hard time finding grants to set up care for the poor.

To fulfill this obligation we started with an idea that was proposed by Don Evans on Yap Island in the Pacific, and that was the "Outer Island Dispensary Program." We had earned some of the money in Guam and the Micronesian Islands, so it was appropriate. The idea here was a low tech program to provide primary care, (see the appendix for a write up of this program). The Foundation set up thirty small, ten by ten foot, hut-like dispensaries, manned by local people who had been trained in family planning, how to immunize children, the use of clean water and promote breast feeding. These were to be used by the people that lived in the village. The dispensary was open 24 hours a day, seven days a week– or at least available by simply getting the attendant to open up and take care of things. They also treated minor infections, parasites, wounds and illness. The local people built the thatched roof waiting area around these small huts. The unit contained a flat examining table and baby scale, a small desk and chair with a cabinet over it with the drugs. FHP supplied generic drugs on a regular basis for free.

This program was so successful that a 50-bed hospital on Yap, which had been overflowing, was reduced in census to between five and ten percent. Infantile diarrhea, which was a big problem, disappeared because the women were encouraged to breast feed and taught how to use clean water if they used formula. We did family planning so there were fewer children to take care of. These centers were a resource within the villages that could be used early on before the people got too sick.

Using this basic model we decided to attempt to set up a program where five small clinics, each manned by a nurse practitioner and an assistant supervised by one managing primary care doctor, would be opened in a low income area of Santa Ana, which was the capital of Orange County, CA. These would be open from 12 noon to 8 pm at night, Tuesday through Saturday, thus making care available at times that low incomes people to get to it. This program would be supported by a budget of about $1.5 million per year from the FHP Foundation and fund raising.

We immediately ran into the problem of our inability to find a manager for this program who understood the problem and was enthusiastic about serving the poor through a new and different type of concept and would take the career risk.

Although there were numerous clinics in this low income area none of them really served the purpose. They were all part time specialty clinics, some open one or two days a week, that did well baby, prenatal, psychiatric, dental, all different little fragments. There was only one that was running as a primary care clinic and that was open the usual 9:00 AM to 5:00 PM when people couldn't get to it.

The other problem was that we didn't realize that Orange County was a very conservative area, resistant to anything new or different. Then the high control reactionary doctors' objective was protecting their income.

In addition, unbeknownst to me there were one or two people on our board, one who was a doctor, who while trying to protect their position as experts in health care, didn't like the idea. Most importantly, it was difficult to find a primary care doctor with management training who would buy into this at the salary we could afford. The lesson learned here is we probably should have paid 50 percent more for the manager and 50 percent more for the doctor, got one of our trained doctor/managers at FHP and one of our trained MBA's from FHP in there on a rotating basis because they were not available in the market– simply not available.   Other obstacles were that the retail space for these clinics for the right size and price was not available. (There is very little retail space in low income areas.) Also the community was not inclined to let us have a special option to use a house, so we had a hard time finding facilities. Therefore it took longer than we had anticipated to find facilities and recruit anybody including the nurse practitioners. So it took about a year to set the program up and it was a little more costly than we had anticipated. But I should have known that because that was what happened to us in Utah.

The program had two purposes. One was to provide services to a population and make them available, assessable and appropriate to the people that could only see the doctor in the evening or on the weekends. Medical care was one portion of this concept. The other was a research program to find out if this system would work and how much money it saved or did not save, in comparison to the cost of the usual fee-for-service system. Identifying the target population and their needs was the third problem.

The other mistake we made was we did not accurately investigate the low income neighborhood and keep these centers just in geographically designated low income neighborhoods making them available for future grants. This partially was the problem of the inability to find the proper facilities to rent in the area that we could modify and use.

By in large however, the program was a success. We found several things that we had not anticipated. The first was that the biggest population at risk and in need was those people with chronic disease between 55 and 65 years old, not yet eligible for Medicare but unable to get private insurance. They were in an age group with a high incidence of chronic problems and no facilities to treat them.

Next we found out that we could save approximately 50 percent of the cost of fee-for-service and be just as effective in providing care. We were not in operation long enough to have any idea how we affected the general health of those people served in the long run.

Unfortunately this program did not survive because of internal warfare amongst the board of directors of FHP Foundation. One of the members, Joe Prevratil, was attempting to make the Foundation his own private fiefdom and it got caught up in the back door take over of FHP. Meanwhile the chief motivator/innovator/chairman was squeezed out so the whole Foundation eventually just fell into a great hole and became just another foundation giving grants to whatever came in over the transom. It was a shame but probably reams could be written on how to avoid such a situation.

GLOSSARY

Adverse Selection: A situation in which, according to insurance company jargon, only the high risk enroll in the insurance program, resulting in higher claim rates and thus causing excessive financial losses.

AHIP (America's Health Insurance Plans): AHIP is the national trade association representing nearly 1,300 member companies providing health insurance or HMO coverage to more than 200 million Americans.

AHA (American Hospital Association): Founded in 1898, the AHA has close to 43,000 individual and organizational members, representing and serving all types of hospitals and health care networks.

AMA (American Medical Association): Founded in 1847, the AMA is the leading professional association of, and advocate for, more than 650,000 physicians in the United States. In the early part of the twentieth century, the AMA was instrumental in creating and implementing standards for physician education.

Capitation: One payment per head. This comes from the Latin root *capit*, meaning *head*. A prepayment for health care services made each month for each contract; i.e., individual.

COBRA (Consolidated Omnibus Reconciliation Act): A government program that mandates health insurance coverage for those who have become unemployed or change jobs. Although it mandates benefits, it does not regulate premium rates so many individuals are priced out of this market. This is another "Band Aid" solution.

Co-Pay: An amount paid by the patient at the time of service, in addition to their monthly premium payment to the insurance company or HMO. The co-pay may be stated as a set amount or as a percentage of the total charged by the provider.

Deductible: The amount of money that must be paid by the individual covered by an insurance policy before an insurance policy begins payment. This can vary from $100 per day in a hospital to $2,000 total, per case, and can be per illness or per year, per individual or per contract.

Exclusions and Limitations: These are usually things that the plan will not cover or will cover only partially. It is very important to know what the exclusions and limitations are. The most usual *exclusion* is obstetrical coverage; some plans can totally exclude coverage for care received out of their service area or for certain procedures or illness (e.g., experimental treatment, some unproven drugs). Even Medicare excludes care outside the United States. *Limitations*, on the other hand, indicate the maximum the insurance policy will pay for a particular service. For example, it may limit the pharmaceuticals covered to generic equivalents, or it may limit how much will be paid for a particular procedure.

GHAA (Group Health Association of America): This was the original prepaid group practice association. The Group IIcalth Association of America eventually merged into an association with the HIAA and became a type of representation for all types of health care coverage.

GREEN MAIL: This is a method of getting rid of a difficult board member or shareholder by offering to buy out their shares at a premium, at 10% to 30%.

HIAA (Health Insurance Association of America): This was an association of most of the major companies that provided health insurance. It has subsequently been merged with Health Plans of America, the former national organization for HMOs.

HMO (Health Maintenance Organization): A term coined by Dr. Paul Ellwood and adopted in conferences held in Jackson Hole, Wyoming. It originally referred mostly to the group practice pre-payment organizations, but later expanded to include IPAs and some insurance company products that posed as HMOs. Legislation in 1973 legitimized the HMO concept.

IPA (Independent Practice Association): This outgrowth of the HMO benefited doctors who were not associated with group practice prepayment organizations but, by forming an IPA, where allowed to sign up and receive payment on a capitation basis or some other modified fee-for-service basis. In return, the capitation limited their fees but not the utilization. Individual physicians were loosely associated with the IPA organization, which supposedly provided some quality control and a list of participating doctors.

Indemnity Insurance: A policy for which an insurance company indemnifies or agrees to pay a set amount for each procedure.

Medicare: A program created during the Lyndon Johnson Administration, on July 30, 1965, to provide healthcare for people over age sixty-five. The federal government, through Social Security, is the universal single payer. In most instances Medicare shops out claims management to the claims departments of insurance companies. Medicare is a federally funded program which pays providers directly for fee-for-service care based upon a fee schedule, but it does not control volume or utilization.

Medicaid (called MediCal in California): A program to provide health care for poor and low-income Americans, Medicaid is a matching program with the states, not a totally federally funded program like Medicare. The federal government matches the money that the states put up for their programs. Originally, states were required only to provide doctor and hospital care. In the more affluent states, they have added services such as prescription drug coverage, dental, long term care, preventive services, and psychiatric services.

PPO (Preferred Provider Organization): Through a loosely held arrangement with an insurance company or IPA, the only obligation of the member doctors is an agreement to discount their inflated fee-for-service schedule. In return, they are listed as available doctors, thus saving the doctors marketing costs but offering no control over utilization.

Premium: The amount of money paid monthly for each individual covered under a health insurance plan.

SCHIP (State Children's Health Insurance Program): A program created under the Clinton Administration to provide care for children of low-income families. This is also a state matching program: the federal government matches what each state pays out annually. Many of the states simply rolled SCHIP into Medicaid; in California it became an insurance company product that attempts to charge poor people a monthly reduced premium for each child – California has considerable money left on the table because even a small monthly premium is too much for most of these families to pay.

Single-Payer: A system in which all fees are paid by one source.

Socialized Medicine: A system in which doctors are employed by the government on salary. The government owns and provides all healthcare facilities and equipment, and citizens may be automatically covered. A current example is our military hospital system, where Army and Navy doctors are paid on government salary and work in hospitals built and administered by the government. The Veteran's Administration is another example of a socialized system.

Stop Loss: A system in which people may continue to get the services but do not make additional payments. In other words, for the consumer, a stop loss is when they pay up to a certain amount, e.g. $5 or $10, for prescriptions and the plan pays for the rest. A stop loss for the insurance company is when the insurance company pays a specific amount, say for a pregnancy, and the patient pays the rest.

Utilization: The volume, amount, and extent of care provided.

SALLY SMITH HUGHES

Graduated from the University of California, Berkeley, in 1963 with an A.B. degree in zoology, and from the University of California, San Francisco, in 1966 with an M.A. degree in anatomy. She received a Ph.D. degree in the history of medicine from the Royal Postgraduate Medical School, University of London, in 1972.

Postgraduate Research Histologist, the Cardiovascular Research Institute, University of California, San Francisco, 1966-1969; science historian for the History of Science and Technology Program, The Bancroft Library, 1978-1980.

Presently Senior Editor on medical and scientific topics for the Regional Oral History Office, and Research Historian in the Department of History of Health Sciences, University of California, San Francisco. Author of The Virus: A History of the Concept, Sally Smith Hughes is currently interviewing in the fields of AIDS and molecular biology/biotechnology.

THERE IS NOTHING MORE DIFFICULT TO
TAKE IN HAND,
MORE PERILOUS TO CONDUCT,
OR MORE UNCERTAIN IN ITS SUCCESS,
THAN TO TAKE THE LEAD IN THE
INTRODUCTION OF A NEW ORDER OF
THINGS.

Niccolo Machiavelli
1469 - 1527

ENDNOTES

[1] Robert Gumbiner, FHP: The Evolution of a Managed Care Health Maintenance Organization, 1955-1992, Regional Oral History Office, University of California, 1994. The oral history is also available as a published book of the same title, but missing two short interviews (with Charles A. Lifschultz and Jack D. Massimino) originally appearing with the oral history.

[2] Robert Gumbiner to Sally Hughes, July 27, 1995

[3] Sally Hughes to Robert Gumbiner, August 21, 1995

[4] Individuals either failed to respond t written requests, explicitly declined participation, or, after initial arrangements for a date and time for telephone interview, were found on multiple attempts to be unavailable.

[5] Robert Gumbiner to Sally Hughes, July 17, 1996

[6] See the first oral history

[7] ##This symbol indicates that a tape has begun or ended. A guide to the tapes follows the transcript.

[8] Robert Gumbiner, M.D., "FHP: The Evolution of a Managed Care Health Maintenance Organization, 1955-1992," Regional Oral History Office, University of California, Berkeley, 1994. Hereafter, Gumbiner oral history I.

[9] For more on this topic, see Gumbiner oral history I

[10] See Appendix A

[11] For more on this topic, see Gumbiner oral history I

[12] For more on this topic, see Gumbiner oral history I

[13] Robert Gumbiner to interviewer, September 20, 1995

[14] Ibid

[15] Robert Gumbiner to FHP shareholders, December 1, 1995. Unless otherwise noted, references are to documents supplied to the interviewer by Gumbiner's office.

[16] Robert Gumbiner to FHP Board of Directors, "FHP; Historical Review and Vision for the Future," June 21, 1995.

[17] Robert Gumbiner to FHP Shareholders, "Concerns with current FHP objectives and long-term shareholder value," December 1, 1995; Robert Gumbiner to "Dear Shareholder," December 28, 1995.

[18] Queen Mary ship project on the Long Beach Waterfront

[19] "A Contrarian View," December 1995, pp. 12-13.

[20] Robert Gumbiner to Jack Anderson, chairman FHP, Int., June 22, 1995; "Chronology of Back-door Takeover of FHP Int (International) by TakeCare (Purchased by FHP)," August 4, 1995.

[21] Robert Gumbiner, KCSA News, June 22, 1995. See appendix.

[22] Salomon Brothers, "FHP International—Restructuring for Consolidation." United States Equity Research, Health Services, October 17, 1995.

[23] For more on the evolution of FHP, see Gumbiner oral history I

[24] Norma Wagner. "FHP Founder Predicts Redesign Will Fail," Salt Lake Tribune, July 17, 1995, pp. F1-F2.

[25] See appendix